English for Cabin Crew

Terence Gerighty
with Shon Davis

Summertown
Publishing

English for Cabin Crew
Terence Gerighty with Shon Davis

Publisher: Nick Sheard

Development Editors: Sally Cooke and Will Capel

Marketing & Communications Manager: Michelle Cresswell

Content Project Editor: Amy Smith

Production Controller: Eyvett Davis

Cover Designer: Starfish

Text Designer: Oxford Designers & Illustrators

Compositor: eMC Design Ltd.

Illustrator: KJA Artists

ISBN: 978-0-462-09873-9

Heinle, Cengage Learning EMEA
Cheriton House, North Way, Andover, Hampshire
SP10 5BE United Kingdom

Cengage Learning is a leading provider of customised learning solutions with office locations around the globe, including Singapore, the United Kingdom, Australia, Mexico, Brazil and Japan. Locate our local office at **international.cengage.com/region**

Cengage Learning products are represented in Canada by Nelson Education Ltd.

Visit Heinle online at **elt.heinle.com**
Visit our corporate website at **cengage.com**

CREDITS

Although every effort has been made to contact copyright holders before publication, this has not always been possible. If notified, the publisher will undertake to rectify any errors or omissions at the earliest opportunity.

Text

The publisher would like to thank the Irish Times and Irish Times Online for permission to adapt and reproduce the article 'Ryanair flight crew's response to take-off incident criticised' by Paul Cullen, Tuesday 15th December 2009, http://www.irishtimes.com/newspaper/frontpage/2009/1215/1224260714345.html

Photos

The publisher would like to thank the following sources for permission to use their copyright protected images:

3 (thumbnail Georgethefourth/iStockphoto.com), 4 (thumbnail Georgethefourth/iStockphoto.com), 6 (thumbnail Georgethefourth/iStockphoto.com), 6 (Brussels Airline), 8 (Alex D'Aquila), 9 (Alexander Demianchuk/Reuters/Corbis), 10 (Shon Davis), 11 (Glow Asia RF/Alamy), 12 (thumbnail Georgethefourth/iStockphoto.com), 15 (Yoz Grahame), 16 (Insadco Photography/Alamy), 18 (Shon Davis), 19a (Chad Ehlers/Alamy), 19b (David De Lossy/Jupiterimages), 20 (thumbnail Georgethefourth/iStockphoto.com), 20 (Jeff Greenberg/Alamy), 21 (courtesy of Thomas Cook Group), 22a (Chris Howes/Wild Places Photography/Alamy), 22b (Ichabod/iStockphoto.com), 22c (Image/Alamy), 23 (easyJet Airline Company Ltd), 26a (Shon Davis), 26b (dbimages/Alamy), 27 (Ingram Publishing/Alamy), 28 (thumbnail Georgethefourth/iStockphoto.com), 29 (BigStockPhoto.com/Bedo), 30 (iStockphoto.com/Vladir09), 31 (Alamy/Alamy), 32a (Images/Alamy), 32b (Shutterstock.com), 32c (Shutterstock.com), 32d (Shutterstock.com), 33a (Shutterstock.com), 33b (Shutterstock.com), 33c (Shutterstock.com), 33d (Greatpapa/Fotolia.com), 34a (Shon Davis), 34b (Ewa Walicka/Shutterstock.com), 34c (LauriPatterson/iStockphoto.com), 34d (bedo/iStockphoto.com), 34e (jirkaejc/BigStockPhoto.com), 35a (Martin Anderson/Alamy), 35b (amana images inc./Alamy), 36 (thumbnail Georgethefourth/iStockphoto.com), 36 (Apis | Abramis/Alamy), 38a (Jeff Greenberg/Alamy), 38b (David R. Frazier Photolibrary, Inc./Alamy), 38c (Arif Ariadi/Getty Images), 38d (gchutka/iStockphoto.com), 40 (Mark Peterson/Corbis), 42a (Shon Davis), 42b (Fernando Soares/Fotolia.com), 43 (The Flight Collection/Alamy), 44 (thumbnail Georgethefourth/iStockphoto.com), 47a (Rafa Irusta/Fotolia.com), 47b (Shutterstock.com), 47c (Nikolai Sorokin/Fotolia.com), 47d (Radu Razvan/Fotolia.com), 47e (Shutterstock.com), 48 (Jiri Rezac/Alamy), 49 (Paul Kane/Getty Images), 50 (Shon Davis), 52 (thumbnail Georgethefourth/iStockphoto.com), 54 (mevans/iStockphoto.com), 55 (Kevpix/Alamy), 56 (Reuters/Brendan McDermid), 58 (Shon Davis), 59 (courtesy of Ethan Smith), 60 (thumbnail Georgethefourth/iStockphoto.com), 66a (Shon Davis), 66b (Reuters/Simon Kwong), 68 (thumbnail Georgethefourth/iStockphoto.com), 68 (Mark Romesser/Alamy), 69 (Jupiterimages/Getty Images), 70a (Peter Grumann/Alamy), 70b (choja/iStockphoto), 72 (Carlos Santa Maria/Fotolia.com), 73 (vario images GmbH & Co.KG/Alamy), 74 (Shon Davis), 75 (mevans/iStockphoto.com), 76 (thumbnail Georgethefourth/iStockphoto.com), 76a (bilderbo/Fotolia.com), 76b (Laif Andersen/Fotolia.com), 78 (British Airways/Alamy), 79 (Image/Alamy), 80a (Shon Davis), 80b (acilo/iStockphoto.com), 81 (Charles Rex Arbogast), 82–121 (thumbnail: Georgethefourth/iStockphoto.com; plane watermark: Mikael Damkier/Fotolia.com)

Printed in China
1 2 3 4 5 6 7 8 9 10 – 15 14 13 12 11

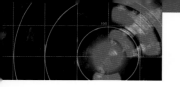

Contents map

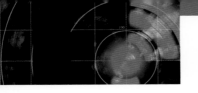

Introduction

English for Cabin Crew is for people working in the aviation industry who want to improve their communication skills, vocabulary, pronunciation and grammatical accuracy. It is designed to be used in class, but you can also use it on your own.

English for Cabin Crew is the perfect companion to the cabin crew training manual. It follows the real-time working routines of flight attendants, from pre-flight briefings to disembarkation, from 'gate to gate'. It follows the operational procedures of the cabin crew and their progress through the different stages of both long-haul and short-haul flights, facing the challenges of boarding, safety demonstrations, serving meals, difficult passengers, possible medical incidents and emergency situations, pre-landing stress, and eventually of reviewing a job well done.

But this book does more. It looks at the special English language used in all these situations. It aims to give flight attendants confidence in using the right English at every stage of the job in hand. So, for example, if you need to know how best to deal with a passenger complaint using the most appropriate English, this book will help you. It will also help you to ask the right questions in a medical crisis and to reply to passengers who are annoying other passengers. It will help you to use appropriate English for routine and non-routine situations on board.

English for Cabin Crew is full of key expressions, of the right thing to say in English on the right occasion. More than this, it presents real job situations and typical passenger and cabin crew exchanges in which the language used is correct, authentic and actual.
➤ The *Listening* section invites you to listen to a real dialogue, and answer questions on it to make sure you fully understand what is happening.
➤ The *Language Focus* explores how to use key expressions in English.
➤ The *Speaking* section provides practice to make you confident of using the key expressions correctly.
➤ The *Reading* and *Vocabulary* sections help to consolidate and build on the language you learn.

Each unit presents a different part of your routine on board. Throughout the book you will find plenty of examples of real situations, plenty of vocabulary, plenty of opportunities for applying what you learn to your own job – all the time speaking and listening to English.

By the time you reach the end of the book, you should be confident about using clear and uncomplicated English to ...
➤ perform all your normal duties on board
➤ address your passengers' problems
➤ handle difficult situations.

Although there may be differences in practices and procedures between different airlines, the use of English and the main communication skills required by flight attendants remain the same. *English for Cabin Crew* will give you the skills to make you a better professional in helping to guarantee the safety and service of your passengers.

What's in *English for Cabin Crew*?

The book has three main sections:
➤ Units 1–10
➤ Case studies
➤ Self Study

Units 1–10

There are ten units, which take you through the routine stages of any flight, long-haul or short-haul. Each unit follows the same pattern: *Listening* and *Language focus* followed by *Pronunciation* and *Speaking* practice. Regular *Vocabulary* sections help build relevant vocabulary and *Reading* texts provide a focus on industry-specific topics.

➤ **Listening** This section sets the scene. You can listen as many times as you want to be sure you understand everything – it's up to you.
➤ **Reading** Comprehension questions and language work act as a springboard to discussion.
➤ **Language focus** Important language structures are highlighted here.
➤ **Pronunciation** You will have the opportunity for essential practice of new words and phrases before proceeding to the *Speaking* tasks.
➤ **Speaking** This section is often a role-play or discussion about an on-the-job situation.

Case studies

There is a *Case study* at the end of each unit. It presents a real incident involving passenger experiences and the actions of cabin crew. The *Case studies* allow you to explore further what you have just learned, taking you from simulation to reality, from practising to experiencing real events. You will be invited to review the content, comment on what happened and discuss what it all means for cabin crew.

You will also hear about the real-life experiences of Shon Davis, a senior cabin crew member with over 20 years' experience. She answers questions relating to the unit subject matter as you progress through the course – about pre-flight briefings, the service on board, medical incidents, emergencies – with fascinating stories of her own experience as a flight attendant.

Self Study

In this section you will find additional practice exercises for independent study.

Study the main unit first, especially the *Listening* sections, so that you become very familiar with the content, vocabulary and language used. Then do the *Self Study* exercises. If you are unsure about any of the vocabulary or language used, don't hesitate to go back to the main unit. Finally, check the answer key and note down your scores.

The *Self Study* pages also contain a 'log book' section. Use this log book page to record your personal progress and your reflections about anything you have studied in the unit.

Audio CD

There is an MP3 Audio CD at the back of the book which contains all the audio material for the course. You can play this on your computer, or you can transfer it to your MP3 player.

Word list

The word list contains key vocabulary from the unit, ordered alphabetically. There is a separate list for each unit, each one including a 'multi-word verb' section as well as additional vocabulary relating to the topic of the main unit. Space is provided for you to write translations into your own language.

Glossary of key expressions

You will find all the phrases and expressions from the *Language focus* sections, as well as other useful phrases from the unit, conveniently listed in the glossary.

Audio scripts and answer key

At the back of the book, ideal for self-study, you will find audio scripts for all the *Listening* and *Pronunciation* exercises, and an answer key.

Tips for self-study

➤ Although the units progress from gate to gate, you do not have to do them in any particular order. You can choose the units that are most relevant to you.
➤ Manage your study time and keep a record of what you have done. Don't spend too long working on a unit without a break.
➤ Revise and review the language you have learned before starting a new unit.
➤ Find a colleague to practise your English with.
➤ Memorize the key expressions in the *Language focus* sections.
➤ Use the Internet to find interesting and relevant articles on aviation topics to develop your vocabulary further.
➤ Create your own vocabulary notebook with translations into your language.

I hope you enjoy using this book and that it helps you in your professional life.

Good luck!

Terence Gerighty

August 2010

Meeting colleagues

 AUDIO 1.1

1 Listen to three cabin crew members, Paola, Tom and Jenny, introducing themselves to each other. The cabin crew are meeting just before the pre-flight briefing. Answer the questions.

1 Where is the flight going to?
2 What does Paola say to introduce herself to Tom?
3 What is Tom's reply?
4 Jenny is not sure of Tom's name. What is her question?
5 Have Jenny and Paola met before?
6 When does the briefing start?

AUDIO 1.2

2 Listen to Paola, Tom and Jenny saying hello to Katrin, another flight attendant. They are on the shuttle for the short ride to the briefing room. Are the statements true (T) or false (F)?

1 Tom and Katrin do not know each other.
2 Paola and Katrin do not know each other.
3 Jenny and Katrin do not know each other.
4 Katrin is not looking forward to going to the US.
5 Paola and Jenny were on a flight to Madrid together.
6 Paola spilled drinks on a passenger.
7 All four are in the same team on the flight.

AUDIO 1.3

3 Listen to the beginning of the cabin crew briefing and answer the questions. The purser starts the meeting. You also hear flight attendants Katrin, Leila and Jutta.

1 What is the name of the purser?
2 Where will Katrin be working on the flight?
3 Where will Leila be in charge?
4 Why is this flight special for Jutta?
5 Who will Jutta be working with?
6 Where will Leila be positioned?

Study these sentences and phrases.

Introducing yourself to someone you do not know
My name's Paola. Pleased to meet you.
Hi there, I'm Tom.

Finding out someone's name
Sorry, what's your name?
Excuse me, could you tell me your name, please?

Introducing other people
This is my colleague, Katrin.
This is Hemal.

Saying hello to people you know or have met before
Hello again, how are you?	Fine thanks. And you?
How's it going?	Very well, thanks.
How are you?	Not too bad.
Hi there!	Hi!

PRONUNCIATION

 AUDIO 1.4

4 Listen and repeat the sentences and phrases in *Language focus*.

SPEAKING

5 Work in groups. Practise all three ways of meeting people.

1 Introduce yourself to someone you are meeting for the first time.
2 Say hello to people you already know.
3 Introduce other people to your friends.

6 Look at the picture and the words in the box. In your groups, discuss what you usually take with you on a flight. What must you never forget to take?

keys ■ passport ■ ID card ■ credit cards ■ mobile phone
toothbrush ■ aspirin ■ MP3 player ■ magazines ■ book

Finding out about the flight

SPEAKING **1** The pre-departure crew meeting is important for several reasons. Put these reasons in order of importance. Discuss your answers with a partner.

_____ to get to know each other
_____ to be told about the coordination of duties
_____ to find out the order of service
_____ to check safety and emergency procedures
_____ to hear about anything special about the flight
_____ to hear about the weather en route

LISTENING AUDIO 1.5

2 Listen to the captain's briefing and answer the questions.

1 Who does the captain introduce first?
2 What is the captain pleased to tell the crew?
3 What does the captain ask Rick Schultz to talk about?
4 What is the possible weather problem on the flight?
5 What should be finished by the time of the weather problem?
6 Because of the weather problem, what will the cabin crew try to do?
7 What does the captain want to make sure of?

VOCABULARY **3** Complete these phrases from the captain's briefing.

1 m_____ turbulence
2 s_____ winds
3 storms o_____ the Atlantic
4 seated and s_____ in
5 the c_____ procedures

LANGUAGE FOCUS
CHECKING AND
CLARIFYING

Study these questions.

Can I just check what the flight time is?
Can you confirm that your crew is familiar with the cockpit procedures?
Can I clarify something?
Can I clarify the time of the meals service?

PRONUNCIATION

 AUDIO 1.6

4 **Listen and repeat the questions in *Language focus*.**

SPEAKING

5 **Work with a partner. Ask and answer questions about what these things mean.**

- seat configuration
- emergency procedures
- special requirements
- passenger load
- turbulence
- 'all clear'
- duties
- schedule

A *What does 'moderate' turbulence mean? / Can I just check what 'moderate' turbulence means?*
B *It means a little bumpy and very unpleasant.*

6 **The first officer warns the crew about the expected stormy weather, which is likely to cause moderate turbulence. Work with a partner. What other kinds of severe weather conditions can affect flights and flight schedules?**

7 **What happens when there is severe weather before take-off? For example, what happens when there are long delays? Have you ever served the meal on the ground?**

8 **If you have to remain strapped in your seat for long periods in the flight because of severe turbulence, do you ...**

a read a magazine?
b chat with passengers nearby?
c plan for when you can continue your duties?
d do something else?

9 **After the briefing, the flight attendants board the aircraft. With your partner, discuss what they have to do on board before the passengers start to arrive.**

Case study

1 Read *A day in the life* opposite and answer the questions.

1 List all the things the flight attendant says she has to check before passengers board the plane.

2 What does she say 'gets a special mention these days'? Why do you think this is?

2 Work with a partner. Answer these questions about pre-flight briefings.

Where?

The briefing in the text takes place on the aircraft. Is there a special reason for this? Is this unusual?

Who?

Who attends the pre-flight briefing?

Who speaks at the briefing? Do the flight attendants only listen?

What?

What sorts of things do they talk about at the pre-flight briefing?

What is the top priority?

Why?

What is the pre-flight briefing for?

Is it really necessary? Aren't all flights the same?

3 With your partner, discuss which of these things are usually mentioned in the pre-flight briefing, and why.

➤ teamwork
➤ introductions
➤ meals service
➤ motivation
➤ leadership
➤ emergency procedures
➤ personal appearance
➤ cockpit entry procedures
➤ safety
➤ responsibilities
➤ special needs passengers
➤ clear task allocation
➤ weather

 AUDIO 1.7

4 Listen to Shon Davis, a senior cabin crew member with over 20 years' experience, as she answers these questions. Make notes about what she says.

1 'What do you remember about your first pre-flight briefing?'

2 'Were these briefings always the same?'

3 'What was the common theme?'

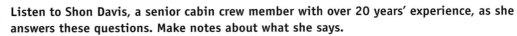

5 Listen again and answer the questions.

1 How did Shon feel on her first pre-flight briefing?

2 What was 'always the same'? What was different?

3 Give details about the different types of passenger she mentions.

6 Work with a partner. Discuss these questions.

1 Why is the pre-flight briefing important for the cabin crew?

2 Do you remember one pre-flight briefing more than all the rest? Why?

3 How do you normally feel during pre-flight briefings? Nervous, excited, relaxed, tense?

A day in the life

> Security and the aircraft's safety features always get a special mention these days.

03.30 Good morning!

My alarm is ringing … already …, and it's time to get up for my flight to Tenerife, which is due to leave at 0700 hours. I get ready, put on my uniform and make sure I have my passport and regular papers neatly tucked away in my carry-on bag. We cabin crew have to check in at least 1 hour and 30 minutes before the aircraft is scheduled to leave, so today that means reporting for work at 05.30. In fact, I'm a little early today (there's no traffic at this time) and I catch the staff shuttle bus to the briefing room.

05.15 Fifteen minutes to the pre-flight briefing

I'm 15 minutes early, which is good, because I've got time to check my cabin crew manual to refresh my knowledge of the all-important emergency procedures and the location of the emergency equipment and exits for today's aircraft, a Boeing 757.

05.30 The pre-flight briefing

Today's pre-flight briefing is being held on the aircraft and the senior crew (usually the purser, although the captain is there too) introduces everyone and takes us through the flight details. Usually this covers the order of the services during the flight, the individual positions and responsibilities for the day, and any special points or passengers with special needs. Security and the aircraft's safety features always get a special mention these days and we're sometimes asked one or two questions about emergency procedures. The captain asks a couple today, and I'm pleased to say that I answer correctly.

06.00 Pre-flight preparations for boarding

This is the time for me and my team to check the emergency equipment and make sure there's a safety instruction card in every passenger's seat pocket. Then we double-check the number of meals on board, the usual drinks trolley and duty-free goods and, of course, stock all the toilets with the necessary hand towels and tissues. All of which leaves just enough time to freshen up and get ready to welcome our passengers on board.

Glossary

tucked away carefully put away
traffic cars, buses, etc. on the roads
a shuttle bus a small bus which travels between an airport and a city
to refresh your knowledge of something to remind yourself about something
to stock to fill with supplies
to freshen up to make yourself clean and tidy

Welcome on board

Welcoming passengers

SPEAKING

1 **Work with a partner. Which of these things do you do just before passengers come on board the aircraft? Which do you do when passengers are actually boarding? When do you do the other things?**

➤ Make sure the aircraft safety instruction cards are in the back of every passenger seat.
➤ Help passengers put their luggage in the overhead lockers.
➤ Check the toilets.
➤ Hurry the passengers to their seats.
➤ Check that your uniform is smart.
➤ Greet the passengers with a smile.
➤ Hand out the arrival immigration forms to complete.
➤ Give special attention to older passengers.
➤ Ask the children not to leave their seats.
➤ Make sure everyone has a blanket.
➤ Check the number of meals.
➤ Make coffee for the flight crew.

2 **Put the duties in order of importance. Compare with your partner.**

LISTENING

 AUDIO 2.1

3 **Listen to the flight attendant, Jenny, welcoming passengers. How many passengers does she greet?**

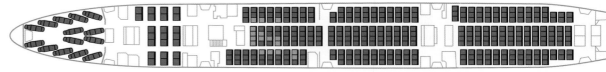

4 **Listen again and complete the sentences.**

1 _____ morning, madam. Welcome on board.
2 _____ I see your boarding pass, please?
3 Hello, _____ are you today, sir?
4 _____ I check your boarding pass?

 AUDIO 2.2

5 **Listen to Jenny welcoming another passenger. What is the problem?**

6 **Listen again and answer the questions.**

1 The plane is full – true or false?
2 What seat number has the woman been given?
3 Why is she upset?
4 When did she request a window seat?
5 What will the flight attendant do?
6 What does the flight attendant ask the passenger to do?

In your opinion, how well does the flight attendant deal with the situation – very well, quite well, or badly?

VOCABULARY

7 Label the boarding pass. Use these words.

> first name ■ family name ■ flight number ■ boarding time ■ gate number
> seat number ■ date ■ airline

What other information is on the boarding pass?

1 _____

2 _____

3 _____

4 _____

5 _____

6 _____

7 _____

8 _____

⑤ SUPER AIRLINES

Boarding closes	15 mins before departure
From HEATHROW	To NY JFK
Service information	KB0931594437

SMITH DAVID JOHN

Carrier SUPER AIRLINES
Name SMITH DAVID JOHN
Boarding Time 11:25
Date 25NOV
Class ECONOMY
Flight HY25 Seat 36B
Gate 18C

Carrier SUPER AIRLINES
Name SMITH DAVID JOHN
Boarding Time 11:25
Date 25NOV
Class ECONOMY
Flight HY25 Seat 36B
Gate 18C

superairlines.com

8 Complete the text. Use these words.

> boarding pass ■ seating arrangements ■ seat number ■ window seats
> check-in ■ overhead lockers ■ in advance ■ hand-baggage (x2)

After [1]_____, passengers proceed to the aircraft with their [2]_____ only. On arrival, they present their [3]_____, which has the [4]_____ on it, to the flight attendant, who will show them where they should go. [5]_____ are made at check-in. Many passengers prefer [6]_____ to aisle seats and often insist on booking them [7]_____. Passengers can ask for help to put their [8]_____ into the [9]_____.

LANGUAGE FOCUS

POLITE REQUESTS

Study these questions.

Can I see your boarding pass?
Can I look at your seat number, please?

Or, more politely:
Could I please see your boarding pass?
Could I check your seat number, please?

Please can I check the seating arrangements?
Please would you sit here for the moment?
Would you follow me, please?
Would you please turn off your mobile phone?
Would you mind just taking this seat until I have
  checked the passenger list?

NOTE

please can be used in all these phrases. It can go at the beginning, at the end, or before the verb.

PRONUNCIATION

 AUDIO 2.3

9 Listen and repeat these sentences and phrases. Remember, welcoming is all about intonation. Speak with a smile in your voice!

1 Welcome on board.
2 Good morning.
3 Good afternoon.
4 Good evening.
5 Hello, how are you?
6 Hello there, how are you today?
7 Could I please see your boarding pass?
8 Would you mind just taking this seat
  until I have checked the passenger list?
9 Can I help you, madam?
10 Can I help you, sir?
11 Would you follow me, please?
12 This way, please.
13 Here you are.
14 Straight across the cabin and turn left.
15 That's right.
16 Carry on down the cabin.

SPEAKING

10 Work with a partner or in small groups. Take turns to role-play welcoming different types of passenger on board and organizing their seating.

13

Settling passengers in their seats

VOCABULARY

1 Label the objects in the cabin. Use these words.

> arm-rest ▪ call button ▪ head-rest ▪ overhead locker ▪ light button
> table ▪ safety instruction card ▪ TV handset control ▪ seatbelt

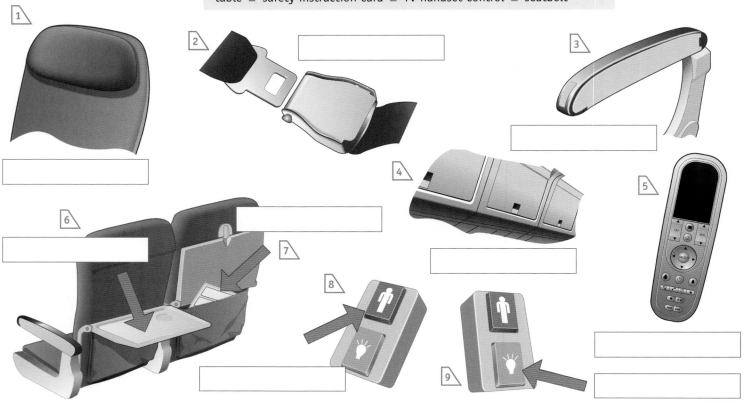

LISTENING

 AUDIO 2.4

2 In *Welcoming passengers* you heard a passenger tell the flight attendant, Jenny, that she wanted to move from a seat in the middle of the row to a window seat. Listen to the rest of the conversation and answer the questions.

1 What does Jenny ask her colleague, Sylvie, for?
2 What does she ask Sylvie's permission to do?
3 What does Jenny offer to do for the passenger?
4 What information does Jenny give the passenger about herself?

How well do you think Jenny dealt with the situation? Would you do the same as Jenny?

  AUDIO 2.5

3 Listen to Jenny greeting another passenger. What is the woman's particular situation?

4 Listen again and answer the questions.

1 When does Jenny say they will need a bassinet for the baby?
2 What two questions does Jenny ask the mother about the baby?
3 How do you think the mother is probably feeling?
4 Where will the baby be seated for take-off?
5 How will the baby be fastened?

What other special situations do you have to deal with when passengers come on board?

LANGUAGE FOCUS

SHOWING HOW
SOMETHING
WORKS

Study these sentences.

Can you show me how it works? (Passenger question)
Of course. / Certainly. (Flight attendant answer)

This is how it works.
First of all, you ... .
Then you ... and ... . (Explanation)

Is that OK / all right with you? (Checking understanding)

The bassinet
First of all, you attach the bassinet to these two clips.
Then you put the baby in **and** attach the cover.
Is that OK?

SPEAKING

5 **Practise explaining how these cabin objects work.**

➤ reclining seat ➤ pull-out table ➤ TV handset control ➤ overhead light

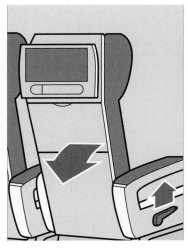
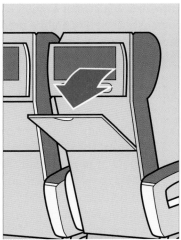
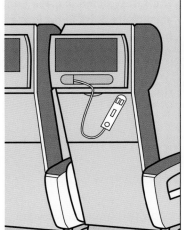
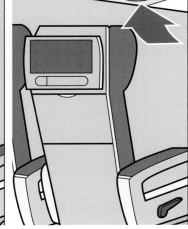

LISTENING

AUDIO 2.6

6 **Listen to Sylvie welcoming the last passenger on board.**
Are the statements true (T) or false (F)?

1 The passenger apologizes for being late.
2 The passenger does not give a reason for being late.
3 Sylvie criticizes him for being late.
4 He is in seat 4F.
5 Jenny checks that everyone is on board.

7 **Listen again and fill in the missing words.**

Sylvie Hello, sir. Welcome on board. May I ¹_____ your boarding pass, please?
Passenger Yes ... ²_____ I'm late. I was delayed ³_____ from the city to the ⁴_____.
Sylvie No problem. We've been ⁵_____ you ... 4F – ⁶_____ to the other side and turn left.
Passenger Many thanks.
Sylvie Jenny, ⁷_____ _____, everyone is on board. Can you check the doors? *(on the interphone)* Tom, doors check, please. OK, prepare for the safety demo.
Jenny OK. Zone C cabin ⁸_____.
Tom OK. Zone D and E cabin secure ...

Demonstrating safety procedures and checking before take-off

This is your captain speaking. Welcome on board. We are almost ready for take-off. Now we request your full attention as we demonstrate the safety features of this aircraft.

READING **1** The safety demo is often done on video, big screen or individual monitors, but flight attendants must know how to demonstrate safety and be prepared to read the safety instructions themselves. Put the instructions below into the correct order. The first and last sentences have been given to help you.

A Ladies and gentlemen, even if you are a frequent traveller, it is important that you listen carefully to the following safety instructions. *1*

B We suggest you keep the seatbelt fastened throughout the flight. ___

C Your life vest is under your seat. This is how you put it on. ___

D There are several emergency exits on this aircraft. They are being pointed out to you now. Please take a few moments now to locate your nearest exit. It may be behind you. If you are sitting in an emergency exit, you must know how to open the door in an emergency and when instructed to do so by the crew. ___

E First, take it out of the pouch and put it over your head. Then pass the straps around your waist and tie them in front. Do not inflate the vest until you leave the aircraft. To inflate the vest, pull on this red cord. Use the whistle and light to attract attention. ___

F If we need to evacuate the aircraft, floor-level lighting will guide you to the exits. ___

G Finally, make sure your seat backs are upright, your tables are folded away and your hand-baggage is either in the overhead locker or under the seat in front of you. ___

H All electronic devices must now be switched off for take-off. ___

I If the pressure drops, an oxygen mask will automatically drop from the compartment above your head. To start the flow of oxygen, pull the mask towards you, put it firmly over your mouth and nose and secure the elastic band behind your head, and breathe normally. If you are travelling with a child or a person who needs assistance, put your mask on first and then assist the other person. ___

J You will find a safety instruction card in the pocket in front of you. Please read this carefully before take-off and familiarize yourself with the emergency exits and procedures on board this Boeing 777S. ___

K In the event of an emergency landing, you will hear 'Brace, brace' and you must adopt this position. Look at the card for the brace position. ___

L When the seatbelt sign is on, you must fasten your seatbelt. To do this, insert the metal fitting into the buckle – like this – and tighten by pulling the strap – like this. To undo the seatbelt, lift the buckle – like this. ___

M We wish you all an enjoyable flight. *13*

LISTENING **2** Listen and check if you got the order right.

AUDIO 2.7

PRONUNCIATION **3** Work with a partner. Take turns to practise reading the safety demonstration text aloud while your partner demonstrates the actions where necessary. Remember, all flight attendants should be able to read the safety instructions clearly, confidently and carefully.

LISTENING **4** Look at the illustrations. What request do you think the flight attendants are making to passengers during final checks?

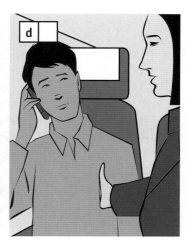

 AUDIO 2.8 **5** Now listen to the flight attendants' requests to passengers. Number the pictures in the order you hear the requests that go with them.

What other requests might you have to make during final checks?

SPEAKING **6** Work with a partner. Practise making requests to passengers during final checks. Use the pictures above to help you, or your own ideas.

Begin with a polite phrase such as *Excuse me ...*, *Please ...*, *Sorry ...* and use *can you* or *could you*.

Excuse me, can you switch off your mobile phone now?

Case study

1 **Read paragraph 1 of** *Bags in bins* **opposite and answer the questions.**

1 What is the text about?
2 Is the description of the last people to board a true one? What happens to their bags?

2 **Read the second paragraph of the text and answer the questions.**

1 Why can boarding often be a difficult and unpleasant experience for all?
2 What do flight attendants ask the passengers to do?
3 What other things should flight attendants be doing while passengers are boarding?

3 **Work with a partner. Discuss these questions about stowing hand-baggage when boarding the plane.**

1 The 'fight for the overheads' seems worse than it used to be. Why do you think this is?
2 Do flight attendants have any control over the situation?
3 Is it better to offer help, or to let passengers manage by themselves?
4 What do most passengers put in their hand-baggage?
5 Is the issue of hand-baggage only a problem on short-haul flights?
6 Does your airline have any rules about the size and weight of hand-baggage? If so, what are they?
7 Do passengers usually respect the rules for hand-baggage?

 AUDIO 2.9

4 **Listen to Shon Davis as she answers these questions. Make notes about what she says.**

1 'Did you enjoy welcoming passengers?'
2 'Did you ever experience any problems when welcoming passengers?'
3 'Do you have any tips for a new flight attendant?'

5 **Listen again and answer the questions.**

1 What three different types of passenger does she mention? What does she say about these three types of passenger?
2 What was the problem with the man she mentions? What difficult decision did she have to make? Did he agree with her decision? What were the consequences of her actions?
3 What is her main recommendation for new flight attendants? What 'little tips' does she also mention?

6 **Work with a partner. Discuss these possible solutions to the problem of hand-baggage. Which do you prefer? Do you have any other ideas?**

➤ The problem has to be solved by the ground crew before boarding.
➤ The number of carry-on bags, their size and their weight has to be strictly controlled.
➤ Airlines have to be tougher.
➤ Check-in has to be stricter.
➤ If hand-baggage is over the permitted size, it has to be checked in.
➤ Make people pay more for carry-on luggage.
➤ Make the overhead lockers bigger.

BAGS IN BINS

When the plane is full, the 'fight for the overheads' is on.

Flight attendants are stressed even before the passengers arrive on board. They know that passengers will arrive with hand-baggage which is too big, too bulky or too heavy, and sometimes with two bags (although only one is permitted), and the fight to fill the bins begins as soon as they are on board. And then there are coats and jackets to put away somewhere, handbags and computer cases, even infant seats and musical instruments. The last passengers to board are often left standing in the aisle with nowhere to put their bags and belongings. If there is no more room to be found, their hand-baggage will have to be off-loaded and put in the hold. It's the law of the jungle. The first to the bins wins.

People become angry and the flight attendants are often

> **It's the law of the jungle. The first to the bins wins.**

caught in the middle. They ask passengers to store small items under the seats, to leave space for others, to free the aisles while others are boarding, but it is becoming more difficult and often more unpleasant. And of course, if crew are stowing passengers' bags, they are not concentrating on their safety duties, checking equipment and passengers' behaviour and needs. This is, after all, a crucial moment before taxiing and take-off with schedules to be respected, too.

Glossary

bins overhead lockers
bulky large, very full
belongings things that belong to someone
hold the part of the aircraft where goods are stored
to stow to put away
crucial extremely important

Making the first announcements

SPEAKING **1** **Work with a partner. Look at the picture and answer the questions.**

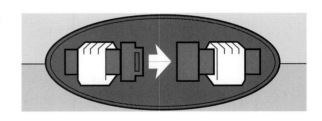

1 What happens immediately after the seatbelt sign is switched off?
2 What do the passengers do?
3 What do the cabin crew do?

LISTENING AUDIO 3.1

2 **Listen to three short announcements from short-haul flights and fill in the missing words.**

1 Ladies and gentlemen, boys and girls, it's great to have you on ¹_____. The seatbelt sign is off, but please don't leave your seats ²_____ you have to. This is only a short flight and we'd like to serve you drinks and snacks as ³_____ as possible. There will only be time for one service and, er ... apologies, we don't have any hot snacks today. ⁴_____ about that. Speak to you again soon.

2 Hello, everyone, this is Stefan speaking. The seatbelt sign is off. Feel ⁵_____ to walk around. We want to serve you drinks shortly, so watch out for the trolley – we don't want to run you down, so don't ⁶_____ the aisles. We don't have a lot of time, so be ⁷_____ with your order, please, and your money, of course. Thanks for your cooperation. Have a good flight.

3 Ladies and gentlemen, the seatbelt sign has been switched off and you can move around the cabin. We shall be coming ⁸_____ the cabin with refreshments in a few moments. Kindly look at the menu card in the pocket in front of you and have your ⁹_____ ready, please. We'd really appreciate it if you had the ¹⁰_____ change for your purchases. Thank you, and enjoy the flight.

3 **Answer these questions about announcements 1–3 in exercise 2.**

1 On which flights is payment for food mentioned?
2 On which flight is there a problem with the food service?
3 On which flight are the cabin crew not in a hurry?

SPEAKING **4** **Answer the questions.**

1 Which of the three announcements is ...
➤ the most fun?
➤ the most serious?
➤ the most friendly?
2 Which announcement do you like the most?

LANGUAGE FOCUS

FORMAL AND INFORMAL LANGUAGE

Study these phrases and sentences.

Formal	Informal
Ladies and gentlemen ...	Hello, everyone.
You can move around the cabin.	Feel free to walk around.
The seatbelt sign has been switched off.	The seatbelt sign is off.
Kindly look at the menu card.	Be ready with your order.

What other formal and informal words or expressions do you know in English?

PRONUNCIATION **5** **Look at these sentences from the announcements in exercise 2. Underline the words which you think are more important and are given extra stress.**

1 It's great to have you on board.
2 Please don't leave your seats unless you have to.
3 We'd like to serve you drinks and snacks as quickly as possible.
4 The seatbelt sign is off.
5 Feel free to walk around.
6 Thanks for your cooperation.
7 We shall be coming through the cabin with refreshments in a few moments.
8 We'd really appreciate it if you had the exact change for your purchases.

 AUDIO 3.2 **6** **Listen and compare your answers. Then listen again and repeat.**

SPEAKING **7** **In groups of three, practise reading aloud the three announcements to each other. Then say them again from memory or short notes.**

Getting started

SPEAKING **1** What are the main differences for flight attendants between long-haul and short-haul flights?

Think about ...
- ➤ the meals and drinks service
- ➤ the facilities for passengers
- ➤ requests from passengers.

LISTENING

 AUDIO 3.3

2 The refreshment service is beginning on a short-haul flight. The flight attendant speaks to four passengers. Listen and answer the questions.

1 What does the first passenger need to do?
2 What does the second passenger want?
3 What does the third passenger want the flight attendant to do?
4 What does the fourth passenger want to know?

3 Listen again to the four conversations and fill in the missing words spoken by the flight attendant.

1 Excuse me, could you _____ down, please?
2 OK, no _____.
3 Yes, of _____.
4 Can I _____ you?
5 Leave it _____ me ...
6 I'll do it as _____ as possible.
7 What can I _____ for you?
8 Listen, don't _____.
9 I'll _____ back to you.

SPEAKING

 4 How well does the flight attendant deal with the four requests? Discuss in groups or with a partner.

LANGUAGE FOCUS

DEALING WITH
PASSENGER NEEDS

Study these sentences.

The flight attendant is polite and helpful:
Can I help you?
What can I do for you?
Yes, of course.
OK, no problem.

The flight attendant is busy, so politely asks passengers to wait:
I'm afraid we're busy just now. Can you wait a moment?
Can you wait until we've finished the service?
Leave it with me and I'll do it as soon as possible.
I'll get back to you. I promise.

PRONUNCIATION

 AUDIO 3.4

5 Listen and practise saying the sentences in *Language focus*. Remember to sound friendly and polite.

SPEAKING

6 Work with a partner. Take turns to practise dealing with passenger problems. Student A is the passenger and Student B the flight attendant.

Student A: Use *I need to / I have to / Could you ...* and these situations.
➤ You want to change your seat.
➤ You need another disembarkation card.
➤ You are very cold.
➤ You are very thirsty.
➤ You have a bad headache.
➤ You are feeling sick.

Student B: Deal with Student A's requests. Use the expressions in *Language focus* to help you.

7 What other passenger needs do you have to deal with at the beginning of the flight? Discuss in groups or with your partner.

Helping to settle passengers

  Work in groups or with a partner. Discuss these questions.

1 What might these types of passenger need to get them settled on a long-haul flight?
➤ passengers travelling alone
➤ groups
➤ families with small children
➤ older people

2 Describe how the passenger types above can sometimes seem. Use these adjectives to help you.

shy ■ nervous ■ unpleasant ■ noisy ■ arrogant ■ demanding

3 Who do you think makes a 'difficult' passenger? Why?

 AUDIO 3.5

2 Listen to the flight attendant speaking to four passengers. In each case, what is the problem?

Passenger 1: _____
Passenger 2: _____
Passenger 3: _____
Passenger 4: _____

3 Listen again. What questions does the flight attendant ask?

Passenger 1: _____
Passenger 2: _____
Passenger 3: _____
Passenger 4: _____

 AUDIO 3.6

4 Practise saying these sentences in a caring and attentive way. Listen and repeat. Try to copy the intonation you hear.

➤ Hello, madam, are you feeling better now?
➤ Can I help you, sir?
➤ Did you call, sir?
➤ Hello there, is everything all right?
➤ No problem, madam.
➤ I do apologize. I'll get it immediately.
➤ You're quite right, sir.
➤ Yes, that's fine. Go ahead.

 AUDIO 3.7

5 Listen to the beginning of the service on a long-haul flight. You will hear four short conversations. Answer the questions.

Conversation 1
1 What does the passenger want to know?
2 How long is the flight?

Conversation 2
3 When will the meal be served?
4 What is the problem with the passenger's children?

Conversation 3
5 What does the passenger ask for?
6 Which channel are the films on?

Conversation 4
7 What does the passenger ask for?
8 Why does the flight attendant put on the call light?

LANGUAGE FOCUS

'COMFORT' EXPRESSIONS

Study these sentences.

Here you are. (*Giving the menu, headphones, blanket, a glass*)
Can I get you anything else?
Anything else I can do for you?
Let me put the call light on (for you).
Don't worry, you'll be fine.
Of course, no problem at all.
I'll be back in five minutes.

PRONUNCIATION

 AUDIO 3.8

6   **Listen and repeat the sentences in *Language focus*.**

SPEAKING

7   **Work with a partner. Look at these different types of passenger. What could you say to help settle them?**

a   an old lady travelling alone
b   a group of happy friends
c   a young man with a guitar
d   a nervous first-time flyer
e   excited children and parents
f   a mother and baby
g   a special needs traveller
h   a quiet elderly couple
i   a woman who is not very well

8   **With your partner, take turns to role-play short conversations with the types of passenger above. Use your own ideas or these suggestions to help you.**

➤ Don't worry, you'll be fine.
➤ Let me help you with that.
➤ Is everything all right?
➤ Can I get you anything, madam?
➤ Is it OK to go in the overhead locker?
➤ If the children are good, I've got a surprise.
➤ Push the call button if you need anything.
➤ Hello, everyone, are you on holiday together?
➤ How are you feeling?

Case study

READING

1 **Read *Flying with children* opposite and answer the questions.**

1 Give examples from the text of the kind of behaviour that can annoy adult passengers.
2 What solutions are proposed or outlined in the text?
3 Do you agree that the action of the purser towards the mother and baby was 'a little harsh'? Why? / Why not?

SPEAKING

2 **Work with a partner. Answer the questions about having young flyers and babies on board.**

1 When you know in advance about young flyers and babies, how do you prepare to settle them into the flight?
2 Why do you think there are so many negative comments from other passengers about them?
3 Is it really the flight attendants' duty to keep the peace?
4 Compare your own experiences of dealing with either young flyers or babies, and of dealing with other passengers' comments and complaints about them.

LISTENING

AUDIO 3.9

3 **Listen to Shon Davis as she answers these questions. Make notes about what she says.**

1 'After take-off, what were your main duties?'
2 'Is there a big difference after take-off on short-haul and long-haul flights?'
3 'Did you have any strange experiences after take-off?'

4 **Listen again and answer the questions.**

1 What does Shon say are a flight attendant's main duties after take-off?
2 What, in Shon's opinion, is the biggest difference between short-haul and long-haul flights? Which did she prefer, and why?
3 What unusual thing did one passenger do during and after take-off? In what other ways could she have handled this incident?

SPEAKING

5 **Work with a partner. Discuss these questions.**

1 After take-off, flight attendants have a duty of customer care for all passengers, including babies. With all your other duties, is there enough time?
2 Do young flyers present the biggest challenge, or are there other types of passenger who give more problems on board? If so, which are they?
3 Are flight attendants on short-haul flights chosen for their speed in performing certain duties, or for other reasons?

Flying with children

A recent survey asked travellers if parents or flight crews should be stricter about the behaviour of young fliers, including babies, on board. Most emailed stories of kids behaving badly and put the blame on permissive parents.

It's true that small children and babies in a cramped cabin can be a nightmare. Here are a few of the responses:

> 'I've had enough of kids who kick the back of my seat while the parent looks elsewhere.'

'I've had enough of kids who kick the back of my seat while the parent looks elsewhere.'

'It drives me insane to be surrounded by families talking loudly and passing food, drink, toys, clothes, etc., back and forth.'

'Families with kids have every right to fly, but they need to respect my rights to a pleasant environment and flight.'

The idea of family-only sections on aircraft was mentioned by many respondents. But families may not enjoy crying babies any more than other passengers.

So what is the role of the crew in keeping peace on a plane? A mother and her screaming baby were recently escorted from a plane because the purser considered that other passengers could not hear the safety instructions announcement. Perhaps that was a little harsh.

'It's a delicate situation,' one experienced flight attendant says. 'If parents don't control kids, flight attendants have to do what they think is best. Every situation is different. Cabin crew can ask parents to control their children, but that is often the beginning of "Mind your own business" or "Have *you* got children?" or "What do you know about kids?" Trying to parent another person's misbehaving child can be quite a problem. In 15 years, I've never had an unruly child on board who was travelling with a hands-on parent.'

Airlines sometimes have cards or colouring books to occupy children on board. A few airlines even provide child-friendly tables and chairs and toys at the gate areas to keep small passengers happy before boarding. And one flight attendant was very clear: 'Kids are members of the public like everyone else, and they often have to go places. I'd always prefer to have ten babies on board than one drunk!'

Glossary

cramped small, with not much space
harsh hard, cruel
unruly badly behaved; difficult to control
a hands-on parent a parent who takes responsibility for their child

Food and drinks

Giving a choice

1 **Read the menu from a long-haul flight and answer the questions.**

  1 Which meals will be served on this flight?

  2 How many courses are there for lunch?

  3 How many choices are there for the main course at lunch?

  4 Do you think this flight departed in the morning, afternoon or evening? Why?

Continental breakfast and lunch

Breakfast
Orange juice, yoghurt, fresh fruit appetizer of seasonal fruit,
croissant served with butter and jam, muffin, tea or coffee

Lunch
Starter

  Seasonal salad with assorted seafood and crunchy garlic bread
  topped with shredded parmesan, accompanied by vinaigrette
  dressing

Main

  Tender pieces of chicken marinated with Arabic spices, cooked
  with rice, tomatoes, cauliflower and garnished with fried onions,
  accompanied by French beans and peas

or

  Charcoal-grilled beef tenderloin, served with a creamy forest
  mushroom sauce topped with chopped chives, accompanied by
  roasted potatoes and red pepper

or

  Vegetable lasagne with a light cheese sauce, accompanied by
  a fresh green salad

Dessert

  A rich dark chocolate mousse, topped with fresh orange and
  strawberries, accompanied by fresh cream

Roll and butter

Tea or coffee with chocolates

2 **Work with a partner. Put food items from the menu into these categories.**

Fruit	Meat and fish	Vegetables and herbs	Dairy food

VOCABULARY   **3**   Label the objects on the meal tray.

1 _____

2 _____

3 _____

4 _____

5 _____

6 _____

7 _____

8 _____

9 _____

10 _____

LISTENING   **4**   Listen to the flight attendant serving the meal to two passengers. Are the sentences true (T) or false (F)?

AUDIO 4.1

1 The man chooses beef.
2 The man chooses white wine to drink.
3 The wine is French.
4 The woman wants fish for her main course.
5 The woman does not like food which is too spicy.
6 The woman asks for the lasagne for her children.
7 There is a problem with the woman's choice for her children.
8 The woman chooses sparkling water to drink for herself and Coke for her children.
9 The flight attendant advises her to pre-order the children's meals for the flight home.

LANGUAGE FOCUS   Study these sentences and phrases.

OFFERING A
CHOICE

Service with a smile
What would you like, sir?
What would you like to drink?
What can I get you, madam?

Giving the meal tray or serving a drink
Here we are, sir.
There you are, madam.

PRONUNCIATION   **5**   Listen and repeat these phrases. Notice the intonation pattern.

AUDIO 4.2

➤ Coffee or tea?
➤ Red or white wine?
➤ Still or sparkling?
➤ Beef or chicken?
➤ Brown or white?
➤ Vegetarian or non-vegetarian?

SPEAKING   **6**   Work with a partner. Take turns to practise ordering and taking orders from the menu. Ask and answer questions about the menu.

A Is the chicken very spicy?   A What are chives?
B No, it's not like a curry.   B They're a kind of herb.

Serving drinks

LISTENING

AUDIO 4.3

1 There are many different kinds of drink which passengers can ask you for during a flight. Listen and repeat this list.

> ~~soda~~ ■ Perrier ■ apple juice ■ ~~Sauvignon Blanc~~ ■ ~~Johnny Walker~~ ■ Merlot
> cognac ■ ~~fruit tea~~ ■ Bloody Mary ■ hot chocolate ■ vodka ■ Martini ■ Kronenberg
> Bacardi rum ■ cappuccino ■ diet Coke ■ lemonade ■ bottled still water ■ port
> Carlsberg ■ Bordeaux ■ champagne ■ tomato juice ■ tonic water ■ Earl Grey tea
> ginger ale ■ bourbon ■ English Breakfast tea ■ espresso

VOCABULARY **2** Now work with a partner and put the drinks in the correct category on the drinks menu.

Drinks Menu	Wines and beers	Spirits
	Sauvignon Blanc	Johnny Walker
	Soft drinks	**Hot drinks**
	soda	fruit tea

Can you add any more items to the menu?

LISTENING **3** Listen to the flight attendant serving drinks to seven passengers. Put the drinks in the order

AUDIO 4.4   you hear them asked for.

a ___ two large glasses of Coke with ice
b ___ a cup of tea
c ___ a pineapple juice
d ___ a large glass of water
e ___ a cold beer
f ___ a gin and tonic
g ___ a vodka
h ___ an apple juice
i ___ a glass of white wine

4 **Listen again and answer the questions.**

1 Does the first passenger want ice with her water?
2 How many different kinds of juice does the flight attendant offer the second passenger?
3 What is the problem with the third passenger's order?
4 How many types of beer does the flight attendant offer the fourth passenger?
5 What does the flight attendant say when she gives the young passenger the Cokes?
6 Does the sixth passenger like the food?
7 Why can't the flight attendant serve the last passenger an alcoholic drink?
8 What does the flight attendant offer instead?

PRONUNCIATION
 AUDIO 4.5

 5 **When serving drinks, flight attendants often have to list the choices. Listen and repeat these lists. Notice the intonation pattern.**

Juices: Apple, orange, pineapple or tomato.
Sodas: Coke, Fanta, Sprite, 7up or Lilt.
Wines: Red wine, white wine, sherry or champagne.
Teas: Earl Grey, English Breakfast, peppermint or green.
Waters: Still water, sparkling water, soda water or tonic water.
Coffees: Espresso, cappuccino, decaffeinated or regular.

SPEAKING

 6 **Work with a partner. Take turns to practise taking orders from the drinks menu you created in exercise 2.**

 7 **What problems can flight attendants have when serving food and drinks to passengers? Add your own ideas to the list and then discuss with your partner, or in groups of three. Do you agree on which are the worst problems?**

➤ The meal isn't hot enough.
➤ The meal is not what the passenger ordered.
➤ The passenger has already drunk too much, but wants more.
➤ Unexpected turbulence causes ...

Duty-free sales

1 **Listen to the announcement and fill in the missing words.**

Ladies and gentlemen, the duty-free sales will ¹_____ shortly. Please prepare your ²_____ of purchases. Check the *Shopping on Board* magazine in your seat ³_____. All prices are in local currency and in US dollars, and you can pay by cash or by ⁴_____ a credit card. We ⁵_____ most major credit cards. Frequent flyers ⁶_____ points on all sales on board. There are some ⁷_____ bargains and there are several items specially designed for our airline.

2 **Find words or phrases in the announcement with these meanings.**

1 soon _____
2 items to buy _____
3 get ready _____
4 airline club members _____
5 discounted items _____
6 created _____

3 **Put the items for sale into the correct category.**

whisky ▪ a brooch ▪ a USB key ▪ face cream ▪ cigars ▪ perfume spray
cognac ▪ aftershave ▪ a soft toy ▪ chocolates ▪ earrings ▪ lipstick
eau de toilette ▪ vodka ▪ a watch ▪ a model aircraft ▪ a scarf
mascara ▪ a travel plug adaptor ▪ a crystal pendant ▪ a travel razor
a bracelet ▪ champagne ▪ a pen ▪ cigarettes ▪ headphones

Perfumes and jewellery	Electric and electronic items	Alcohol and tobacco	Cosmetics	Gifts

What other duty-free items can you add to the categories?

LISTENING
 AUDIO 4.7

4 **Listen to a passenger buying some duty-free goods and answer the questions.**

1 What does the passenger want to buy for his daughter?
2 How much does he pay for his daughter's present?
3 What else does the passenger buy?
4 How does he pay for his purchase?
5 Why does the passenger give the flight attendant two cards?
6 What does he need with his purchase?

LANGUAGE FOCUS
MONEY
TRANSACTIONS

Study these sentences and phrases.

The perfume costs 41 dollars.
The scarves are 72 dollars each.
Forty-one plus [+] 72 makes 113 dollars.
Four times [x] eight equals [=] 32 dollars.
A hundred dollars minus [–] 85 – that's 15 dollars change.
That comes to 120 euros.
How will you be paying? By card or with cash?
How would you like to pay?
Here's your receipt, your card and your gifts.

PRONUNCIATION
 AUDIO 4.8

5 **Listen and repeat the sentences in *Language focus*.**

SPEAKING

6 **How good are you at counting money and adding up a total for your passengers? Work with a partner. Fill in the totals below, then practise saying the sentences.**

1 $19.50 + $27.00 = _____
2 $20 – $11.75 = _____
3 €43.00 + €13.75 = _____
4 €6.75 x 2 = _____
5 £11.45 x 2 = _____
6 $33.39 + $7.20 = _____

7 **What is the currency in these countries?**

➤ Spain ➤ China ➤ Australia ➤ Brazil ➤ Singapore
➤ Saudi Arabia ➤ Russia ➤ United Arab Emirates ➤ Nigeria ➤ Pakistan

8 **What is your local currency? What is the rate of exchange with the Japanese yen, the US dollar and the euro?**

9 **With your partner, take turns to practise buying and selling duty-free goods from the vocabulary list. Make up prices for the items.**

A I'd like some mascara please.
B Certainly, madam. The mascara costs …

10 **Which duty-free goods are most in demand by passengers? Is it the same on all flights, or are there differences? Discuss with your partner or in small groups.**

Case study

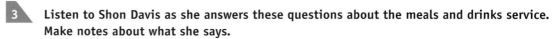

1 **Read the different opinions and experiences of in-flight food opposite and answer the questions.**

1 Which of the opinions and experiences 1–10 are those of passengers (P), and which of crew (C)? Which could be either (E)?
2 Which express a positive opinion about the food service on board, and which a negative opinion? Which do not express an opinion?
3 Underline all the adjectives and phrases used to describe food in the texts. Do they have a positive or negative meaning?

SPEAKING **2** **Work with a partner. Answer the questions and discuss the in-flight food on both long-haul and short-haul flights.**

1 In your experience, are passengers difficult to please when it comes to in-flight food? If so, why? What do they complain about most?
2 Are the problems usually with the quality of the service provided by the flight attendants, or the quality of the food itself?
3 Is the solution to have one excellent meal on long-haul flights, and no food at all on short-haul flights? If not, why not?
4 What improvements would you like to suggest to your airline?

LISTENING AUDIO 4.9 **3** **Listen to Shon Davis as she answers these questions about the meals and drinks service. Make notes about what she says.**

1 'Did you enjoy this part of the flight?'
2 'How much do cabin crew know about the meals in advance?'
3 'Do you remember one special incident during the meals service?'

4 **Listen again and answer the questions.**

1 Why did she especially enjoy the meals and drinks service? Why was this the 'nicest part' of the in-flight service?
2 When are cabin crew told about the meals? What exactly are they told?
3 Can you retell the story of the special incident she remembers so well? How was this problem solved? Was this a good solution to the problem?

SPEAKING **5** **Work with a partner. Discuss these questions.**

1 Airlines spend a lot of money on food. Why do you think this is? Are they successful in what they are trying to do?
2 What do you think about meals for the crew on board? Are these adequate?
3 'Bar snacks on short flights are insulting, over-priced and tasteless, and meals on most long-haul flights are bland, poorly presented and served without grace.' Do you agree with this comment?

File　Edit　View　Favorites　Tools　Help　Links　➤

Airline food...
your thoughts...

1   Added 08 October 08:26

The in-flight meal was fine. We were offered a choice and a selection of drinks. There was no rush. The flight attendants even found time to chat a little and make the whole experience enjoyable. I'll definitely travel on this airline again.

2   Added 05 October 11:12

That was the worst meal I've ever had. It was served in a box with a plastic fork and put on my tray table without a word or a smile. Even now, I'm not sure what it was.

3   Added 03 October 19:52

If you're in Business class, you're fine. The meals are well prepared, look great and taste even better. In Economy, it's the opposite. The meal is bland, not very hot, badly presented and tasteless. It's better to take your own food on board. At least you can eat it.

4   Added 03 October 17:30

The airlines long ago realized that their job – their product, and what people pay them for – is transportation, not food service. Some day the flying public will realize that, too.

5   Added 01 October 12:56

An aircraft is not a flying restaurant.

6   Added 28 September 20:17

I am a flight attendant for a major international airline. I've been flying for nearly thirty years, and in that time people have always complained about airline food. I honestly think passengers are being unrealistic. This is a ride in an aircraft, not a trip to a top-class restaurant. It is what it is. It's not going to get any better either, with internet fares and the present state of the airline industry.

7   Added 22 September 08:48

Yes, yes, yes, it's been said a million times before: the food on planes, even in the front of planes, is dreadful.

8   Added 20 September 17:36

I want to point out that of all the dreadful food in the world, perhaps no dreadful food is presented with more ridiculous fanfare than the dreadful food in the sky.

9   Added 13 September 18:15

On a recent trip I had the misfortune to buy a snackbox. It was not fit for human consumption unless you were alone in the Arctic or lost in the jungle.

10   Added 10 September 10:42

I fly quite a bit, and to be honest I've never had a bad meal. I am much more irritated when there is no complimentary food at all.

Glossary

bland tasteless
dreadful very bad
a fanfare a big display
not fit for human consumption not good enough for people to eat
complimentary free

Minor passenger problems

Identifying passenger problems

SPEAKING

1 As a flight attendant, you are expected to deal with all sorts of problems, for example an in-flight entertainment handset that doesn't work.

Work in pairs or small groups. Make a list of other regular, minor passenger problems you can have on flights.

LISTENING

AUDIO 5.1

2 Listen to a flight attendant dealing with two passenger problems and answer the questions.

1 What can't the first passenger do?
2 Is his handset broken?
3 Does the flight attendant fix the problem?
4 Does the second passenger want to watch a TV programme or a film?
5 Does the flight attendant fix the problem?

LANGUAGE FOCUS

FINDING OUT
THE PROBLEM

Study these questions.

Did you call, sir?
What's the problem?
What's the matter?
How can I help (you)?

PRONUNCIATION

AUDIO 5.2

3 Listen and repeat the flight attendant's questions. Notice how the intonation goes up at the end in the yes/no questions (1–3), and down in the open questions (4–6).

1 Did you call, sir?
2 Your handset?
3 OK?
4 What's the problem?
5 What's the matter?
6 How can I help?

LISTENING

 AUDIO 5.3

4 Listen to four exchanges between passengers and flight attendants. All the passengers have pushed the call button.

Which of these are the four problems? Number them in the order you hear them.

a _____ a sick child
b _____ an angry man
c _____ a crying baby
d _____ a cold passenger
e _____ a hungry passenger
f _____ a noisy group
g _____ a troublesome neighbour
h _____ a nervous elderly lady
i _____ a worried traveller
j _____ a thirsty teenager

SPEAKING

5 The flight attendant has many different roles. Work with a partner. Which of these roles best describes the flight attendant in the problem situations in audio 5.3 above?

Can you think of any other roles a flight attendant might have?

> diplomat ■ firefighter ■ referee ■ bank clerk ■ nurse ■ waiter(ress)
> nanny ■ lifesaver ■ police officer ■ receptionist ■ friend ■ information officer

6 Now discuss these questions with your partner or in small groups.

➤ Which are the two most important roles, in your opinion?
➤ Which are the two least important?
➤ Which roles do you most commonly take?
➤ What other roles do you sometimes take?

Dealing with problems

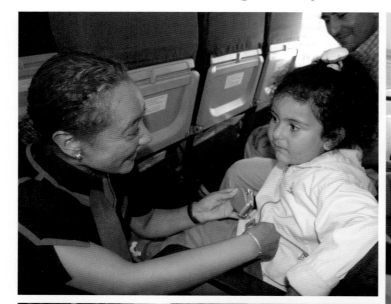

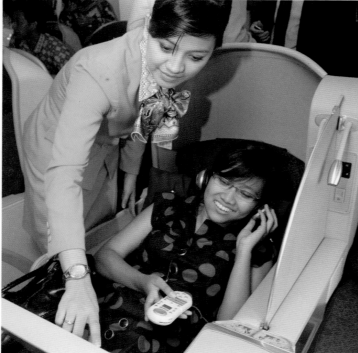

1 Look at the photos. What do you think the flight attendants are saying to these passengers?

 AUDIO 5.4

2 Listen to how the flight attendants solved the four problems you heard in *Identifying passenger problems*, exercise 4. Answer the questions.

1 What does the flight attendant offer to do for the worried traveller?
2 What does the flight attendant agree to get the hungry passenger?
3 What does the flight attendant offer to get the cold passenger?
4 Can the flight attendant get the sick child some paracetamol?
5 What does the flight attendant offer to do for the passenger with the sick child?

3 **Listen again to the four conversations and complete the sentences.**

1 I'll check on our arrival time and _____ to you.
2 I'll _____ it for you. A sandwich or pot noodles?
3 I'll get you a blanket in the _____, if you'd like.
4 I'll _____ what I can do.
5 I'll _____ if there is a doctor or nurse on board.

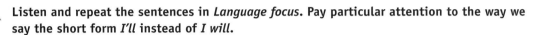

LANGUAGE FOCUS

OFFERING TO
HELP (1)

We use *will* to make an immediate offer to do something. Study these sentences.

Offering to do something for a passenger

I'll check on our arrival time and get back to you.

I'll ask if there is a doctor or nurse on board.

I'll get you a blanket.

I'll get it for you.

I'll get it now.

I'll show you how it works.

I'll get you another one.

PRONUNCIATION

 AUDIO 5.5

4 **Listen and repeat the sentences in *Language focus*. Pay particular attention to the way we say the short form *I'll* instead of *I will*.**

SPEAKING

5 **Work with a partner. Take turns to practise dealing with passenger problems. Use the diagram below to help you.**

The problems:
➤ The video screen doesn't work.
➤ A baby is crying.
➤ The reading light goes on and off.
➤ A neighbour's music is too loud.
➤ You can't sleep because of a noisy group nearby.
➤ You can't open the overhead locker.
➤ The toilet is dirty.
➤ The seat cushion is wet.
➤ The headset is broken.

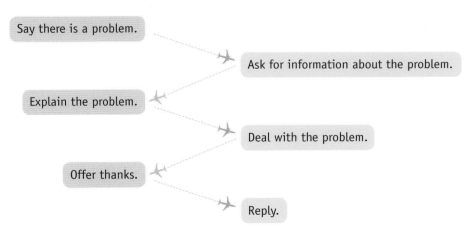

Saying sorry

SPEAKING

1 **Work with a partner or in small groups. Discuss these questions.**

➤ How often do you have to apologize to passengers on a flight?

➤ What are some of the things you have to apologize for?

➤ What makes passengers angry?

➤ How do you make them *less* angry? Do you make excuses or give reasons for the problem? Or do you just apologize?

LISTENING

 AUDIO 5.6

2 **Listen to the flight attendant serving drinks and snacks to four passengers. As you listen, make a note of three things the flight attendant has not got today.**

3 **Listen again and answer the questions.**

1 Which passenger is the most angry about the situation?

2 To which passenger does the flight attendant give a reason or excuse for the problem?

3 How many times does the flight attendant use the word *sorry*?

4 How many times does the flight attendant apologize?

 AUDIO 5.7

4 **Try to fill in the missing words in this extract from the Listening. Then listen and check your answers.**

Flight attendant	What can I ¹_____ you, sir?
Passenger	Two cheese ²_____ and two diet Cokes, please.
Flight attendant	Oh dear, I *am* sorry, but we've ³_____ out of cheese. They've been very ⁴_____ today. But I can offer you ⁵_____ sandwiches.
Passenger	I don't believe it – it's the ⁶_____ old story. You always ⁷_____ to run out.
Flight attendant	Once again, I can only ⁸_____, sir. Would you like the chicken?
Passenger	No ⁹_____, no thank you.
Flight attendant	Sorry ¹⁰_____ that.

LANGUAGE FOCUS

APOLOGIZING

NOTE

Sorry is often followed by *madam* or *sir*: *I'm sorry, madam. / Sorry, sir.*

Study these sentences.

Sorry, we don't have any peppermint – my mistake.
I'm afraid we've only got apple juice and orange juice today.
I do apologize.
I am sorry, but we've run out of cheese.
I can only apologize, sir.
Sorry about that.
I'm really sorry, we haven't got any left.

PRONUNCIATION

 AUDIO 5.8

5 **It is very important to sound apologetic when you say you are sorry. Listen and repeat these sentences from *Language focus*, stressing the words in bold. Try to copy the wide range of intonation.**

➤ **Sorry**, we don't have any peppermint – **my** mistake.
➤ I'm **afraid** we've **only** got **apple** juice and **orange** juice today.
➤ I **do** apologize.
➤ I **am** sorry, but we've run out of cheese.
➤ I can **only** apologize, sir.
➤ **Sorry** about that.
➤ I'm **really** sorry, we haven't got any left.

SPEAKING

6 **Work with a partner. Take turns to practise apologizing for problems. You can use the ideas below or your own ideas. Try to give a reason or excuse for the problem. Use the diagram to help you.**

The problems:
➤ The cabin is too hot.
➤ There isn't a vegetarian option on the menu.
➤ The choice of in-flight movies is poor.
➤ The seats are uncomfortable.

Passenger   Flight attendant

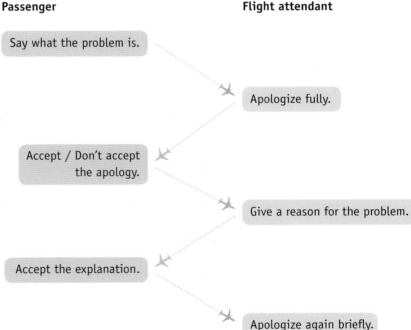

Say what the problem is.

Apologize fully.

Accept / Don't accept the apology.

Give a reason for the problem.

Accept the explanation.

Apologize again briefly.

Case study

Read *Pickpocket strikes on flight from Tokyo to Paris* opposite and answer the questions.

1 What exactly happened on board this flight?
2 How many passengers were affected, and in which part of the aircraft?
3 Did the airline spokesperson admit any responsibility for what happened?

SPEAKING

2 Work with a partner. Discuss these questions.

1 How could such a serious theft happen in a secure environment? Could the cabin crew have done anything to prevent it?
2 Do you think it is the responsibility of the airline to find stolen cash and belongings? What about finding the thief? What is your airline's policy?
3 Make a list of five common problems which you can usually solve. Think of two problems you were not able to solve. Why not?
4 What is the most unusual problem you have experienced on a flight?

LISTENING

AUDIO 5.9

3 Listen to Shon Davis as she answers these questions. Make notes about what she says.

1 'In general, are passengers difficult to please?'
2 'What's the most common minor complaint?'
3 'Is the passenger always right?'

4 Listen again and answer the questions.

1 How much customer service training do most airlines provide?
2 What are the two most common complaints Shon mentions? Is this also your experience?
3 Even if you think a passenger is wrong about something, what is it important that you do?

SPEAKING

5 Work with a partner. Discuss these questions.

1 The pickpocket problem was unusual, but in general is it the flight attendant's job to make sure that passengers' problems are always solved?
2 How do you feel as you board your flights knowing that you are likely to have passenger problems? Tense and nervous? Or do you look forward to the challenge?
3 Do you agree with Shon about seating being the most common passenger problem? Give reasons for your answer.

Pickpocket strikes on flight from Tokyo to Paris

A pickpocket stole thousands of pounds' worth of cash from Business class passengers as they slept on a flight from Tokyo to Paris.

Cabin crew did not spot the thief at work as he went through wallets and handbags during the 12-hour overnight flight.

Passengers woke to find large sums of cash missing. The captain alerted police, who met the Boeing 777 jet as it landed at Paris Charles de Gaulle airport on Tuesday morning, but they were unable to identify the thief.

One passenger told police that about £3,000 in mixed currencies had vanished from her handbag.

Five others, who had paid up to £5,000 each for their tickets, said they had also lost thousands in cash.

One told the French news website *Le Post*: 'Most long-haul travellers sleep on overnight flights like this. But at the prices we pay for tickets, you would expect the cabin crew to be watching over us and making sure our belongings are safe.'

A spokesperson for the airline said it could not comment on this particular incident, but added: 'As a general rule, passengers' belongings in the cabin are their responsibility, while luggage in the hold is the airline's responsibility.'

> At the prices we pay for tickets, you would expect the cabin crew to be watching over us and making sure our belongings are safe.

Glossary

a pickpocket someone who steals from people's bags and pockets
to spot to notice
a thief someone who steals things
a wallet pocket-sized holder for money
large sums of cash large amounts of money
to alert to warn someone, to make someone aware
to vanish to disappear
the hold the place where large suitcases are stored in a plane

Is there a doctor on board?

Dealing with an on-board accident

1 **Work with a partner or in small groups. Discuss these questions.**

➤ What kinds of accident requiring medical attention can happen to both cabin crew and passengers on a flight? Make a list.

➤ What is the worst on-board accident you have seen or experienced?

➤ What first aid are you qualified to carry out? What are you not qualified or not allowed to do?

2 **Listen to flight attendants Leila and Hemal dealing with an on-board accident and answer the questions.**

1 Who has been injured?

2 What kind of injury does the person have?

3 What caused the accident?

4 What does Leila ask the male passenger to do?

5 What does Leila ask Hemal to do?

AUDIO 6.2

3 **Listen to what happens next and answer the questions.**

1 Who is the injured passenger travelling with?

2 How is she feeling?

3 What does Leila offer her?

4 What has the injured passenger got on her forehead?

5 What does Leila say she is going to do?

6 What two things does Leila want the injured passenger to do?

4 **Complete the missing words in these sentences from the two Listenings.**

1 This lady's been h_____. She's b_____.

2 A laptop f_____ onto her head.

3 How are you f_____?

4 You've had a nasty b_____ on your head.

5 I'll put a d_____ over it.

6 I was a bit d_____, but I'm fine now.

7 Can you h _____ this compress against your forehead?

LANGUAGE FOCUS

CHECK → CALL
→ CARE

Study these sentences.

Check → Call → Care is the standard response to medical problems on board.
Check (Find out what is wrong)
Do you have any pain?
Do you feel well enough to sit up?
How are you feeling?
Call (Describe, inform and get help)
I need some help.
Get the first aid kit immediately.
Can you get her a glass of water, please?
Care (Take action and take care)
I'm going to clean up the wound and put a dressing over it.
Can you hold this compress against your forehead?

PRONUNCIATION

AUDIO 6.3

5 **Listen and repeat these questions from the Listening sections. Remember the intonation for open questions (⌐) and yes/no questions (⌐).**

➤ What's happened?
➤ Are you all right?
➤ Can you hear me?
➤ How are you feeling?
➤ Do you have any pain?
➤ Do you feel well enough to sit up?
➤ How is she?
➤ Can you hold this compress against your forehead?
➤ Can you get her a glass of water, please?

VOCABULARY

6 **Label the items in the emergency medical kit. Use these words.**

stethoscope ■ syringes ■ dressings ■ gloves
aspirin ■ cardiopulmonary resuscitation (CPR) mask
automatic external defibrillator (AED) ■ bandages
oxygen ■ antiseptic wipes

1 _____

2 _____

3 _____

4 _____

5 _____

6 _____

7 _____

8 _____

9 _____

10 _____

Dealing with a serious medical incident

SPEAKING **1** **Work with a partner or in small groups. Discuss these questions.**

➤ Apart from accidental injuries, what other kinds of medical problem have you had to deal with on flights? Make a list of major and minor incidents.

➤ What is the most serious on-board medical incident you have had to deal with? What happened?

LISTENING

 AUDIO 6.4

2 **Listen to Rani, Bilal and Safiya dealing with a major medical incident on a flight from Delhi to Colombo. Are the sentences true (T) or false (F)?**

1 The sick passenger is unconscious.
2 The sick passenger is travelling alone.
3 Rani wants to put the sick passenger in a seat.
4 The sick passenger has collapsed before.
5 Rani and Bilal give the sick passenger oxygen.
6 Rani and Bilal can deal with the situation themselves.
7 The sick passenger is on medication.
8 The sick passenger is 53 and in good health.
9 Safiya tells Anton, the purser, about the situation.
10 There isn't a doctor on board.

VOCABULARY **3** **Complete these sentences from the Listening. Listen again if necessary.**

1 Can you h_____ me?
2 I think he's had a h_____ attack.
3 He's not b_____.
4 Let's g_____ him on the floor.
5 Help me get the m_____ over his head.
6 We're taking c_____ of him.
7 We a_____ CPR for two minutes.
8 His p_____ is very weak.

SPEAKING

 4 How well did Rani and Bilal follow the Check → Call → Care procedure? Discuss with a partner or in small groups.

LANGUAGE FOCUS
GIVING
INSTRUCTIONS
TO CREW

Study these instructions.

Bilal, grab the oxygen.
Get Safiya to call Anton.
Help me get the mask over his head.
Tell the captain.
Make an announcement immediately.

PRONUNCIATION

 AUDIO 6.5

5 Listen and repeat the instructions in *Language focus*.

LISTENING

 AUDIO 6.6

6 Listen to Anton, the purser, speaking to the captain about the sick passenger. Answer the questions.

1 What's the doctor's diagnosis?
2 Is the passenger in danger?
3 What has the doctor requested?
4 What action does the captain say he will take?

 AUDIO 6.7

7 Try to fill in the missing words in this announcement the captain makes. Then listen and check your answers.

Ladies and gentlemen, this is an ¹_____ announcement. We have a serious medical situation on board and we need to ²_____ to Mumbai, the ³_____ airport, as soon as possible. The flight attendants will now ⁴_____ the cabin for landing. I ⁵_____ being on the ground within the next 15 minutes. After landing at Mumbai, you must ⁶_____ on board the aircraft. I do apologize for any ⁷_____ this diversion may cause. However, I'd like to thank you for your cooperation and understanding. After landing at Mumbai, we will keep you regularly ⁸_____ with our plans for your continued flight today.

PRONUNCIATION

 AUDIO 6.8

8 Listen and practise reading aloud this short announcement.

'Ladies and gentlemen, if there is a doctor on board, please make yourself known to a member of the crew immediately by pressing your call bell. Thank you.'

SPEAKING

9 Work in small groups. Role-play a medical emergency where two of you are flight attendants and two of you are passengers. Then swap roles. Remember to follow the Check → Call → Care procedure.

A What's happened?
B It's my husband, he's feeling ill.
C Are you on any medication, sir?
D Yes, I take pills for my heart …

Reporting a medical incident

SPEAKING

1 After the flight, you tell a colleague what happened in *Dealing with a serious medical incident*. Work with a partner and take turns to role-play the conversation.

A *Did you hear about our flight yesterday?*
B *No, what happened?*
A *Well, ...*
B *Really!*

LANGUAGE FOCUS

TALKING ABOUT
THE PAST

Study these sentences.

What happened?	He collapsed. He stopped breathing,
What was the problem?	He had a heart attack.
What did you do?	We gave him oxygen and administered CPR.
Was there a doctor on board?	Yes, thank goodness, he arrived almost immediately.

PRONUNCIATION

2 Put these verbs in the correct column according to how the endings are pronounced.

~~wanted~~ ■ ~~collapsed~~ ■ ~~loosened~~ ■ happened ■ checked ■ reported
fainted ■ resumed ■ informed ■ stopped ■ needed ■ arrived
closed ■ remained ■ decided ■ asked ■ administered ■ suffered
switched ■ assisted ■ recommended

/t/	/d/	/ɪd/
collapsed	loosened	wanted

 AUDIO 6.9   **Listen and check your answers. Then listen again and repeat.**

VOCABULARY

3 Make sentences using the verbs from exercise 2 to show you understand them. Try and make sentences in the context of medical incidents or on-board accidents.

The passenger collapsed during the flight.

LANGUAGE FOCUS

LINKING WORDS

Study these sentences.

At the beginning / At first the turbulence wasn't too bad.
Soon after / Then it started to get worse.
In the end / Eventually we had to stop the meals service.

First we fetched the first aid kit, and **then / after that** we cleaned the wound.
Finally we put a dressing on it.

SPEAKING

4 Think about the on-board accident in the Listening on page 44. Take turns to role-play a conversation telling a colleague what happened. Use verbs from exercise 2 and linking words from *Language focus* to tell the story.

READING

5 Complete the report form about what happened in *Dealing with a serious medical incident*. Use these words.

> transferred ■ pulse ■ cardiac ■ resumed ■ first ■ condition
> comfortable ■ services ■ defibrillator ■ recommended ■ happened
> administer ■ aware ■ until

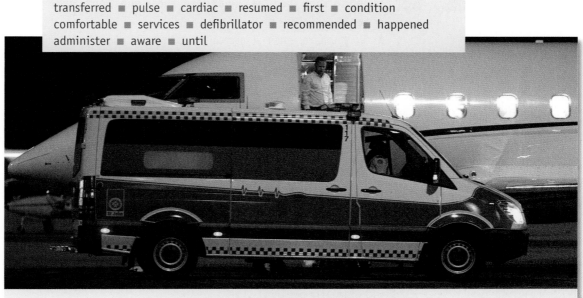

**Report on Medical Incident on Flight IC321
from Delhi to Colombo**

The incident ¹_____ at 16.40, that is, two hours into the flight.

A male passenger aged 63 suffered a ²_____ arrest.

Two flight attendants assisted the patient as soon as the alarm was raised and immediately checked the man's ³_____, made him ⁴_____, took his ⁵_____, checked his medical history with his wife who was travelling with him, got the oxygen and a ⁶_____ and informed the purser. The purser informed the captain. The flight attendants gave prompt ⁷_____ aid and then began to ⁸_____ CPR. Fortunately there was a doctor on board and he said the man had suffered a cardiac arrest and was in a serious condition. The doctor ⁹_____ immediate hospitalization. The captain decided to land at Mumbai, the closest international airport. The captain made an announcement to make passengers ¹⁰_____ of the situation. He also requested ATC to provide full medical emergency ¹¹_____ on arrival. The doctor remained with the patient ¹²_____ landing.

The plane landed at 17.01 and the emergency services took charge of the patient, who was ¹³_____ to hospital. The flight ¹⁴_____ at 18.10.

It was later reported that the patient was in a stable condition in hospital in Mumbai.

Case study

READING

1 Read *Is there a doctor on board?* opposite and answer the questions.

1 What happened on this transatlantic flight?
2 How many passengers did the doctor see? Were these serious medical emergencies?
3 What was the role of the flight attendants during the medical crises?
4 What is your opinion of the doctor and his behaviour on this flight?

SPEAKING

2 Work with a partner. Answer the questions and discuss the medical incidents.

1 Discuss the actions of the flight attendants in the incidents.
2 What kind of medical training have most flight attendants had?
3 What do you think would have happened if no doctor had been on board?

LISTENING

 AUDIO 6.10

3 Listen to Shon Davis as she answers these questions. Make notes about what she says.

1 'Were you trained to be a good nurse?'
2 'Do you have a special medical crisis that you remember in particular?'
3 'What's your advice about medical incidents on board to flight attendants in their final phase of training?'

4 Listen again and answer the questions.

1 Complete this extract. Did your first-aid training cover the same things?
'... we cover all sorts of things from ¹_____ to ²_____, to ³_____
_____ and ⁴_____, and we are taught how to deal with such a wide range of
situations that can occur on board, you know, from ⁵_____ _____ on board to,
you know, a ⁶_____ _____, so there are many different aspects of nursing training
that flight attendants receive ...'
2 Work with a partner to retell Shon's story of the medical crisis. Use these words and expressions.
➤ sweating profusely
➤ a glass of water
➤ the food trolleys
➤ recovery position
➤ one of the stewardesses
➤ oxygen bottle
3 Why does Shon say you should not worry too much about in-flight incidents?

SPEAKING

5 Discuss these questions.

1 Is your first aid training 'very, very good', or do you rely on more experienced colleagues when medical incidents occur?
2 Is training for medical incidents the most important part of your training? What personal qualities are needed for dealing with medical incidents?
3 Life-threatening incidents are rare during flights. Do you know of any? What happened?

Is there a doctor on board?

Most people who have flown long-distance flights have heard the call: 'If there is a medical doctor on board, please identify yourself to a flight attendant.' But, believe me, if you're a doctor, your first instinct is to hide in the toilet. I know this sort of thing should be second nature to me, but I'm used to working in a hospital with a very small audience. In Economy class, there can be 300 people watching, who are very interested in what's going on. So, when I heard the call, somewhere over the mid-Atlantic, I tried to sink deeper into my seat, hiding my face behind my magazine. But, when nobody else responded, I pushed the call button.

There was a male passenger in First class with abdominal pain. He was 60 to 70 years old. I performed a brief examination and I concluded that the pain was probably a kidney stone. I gave the man some pain killers and said I'd check on him later.

I tried to sleep, but maybe an hour later the attendant approached me again. 'There's another patient for you.' Oh dear! He was also an elderly man with a history of heart disease. I asked the attendant if there was a defibrillator on board. This second patient said he had typical chest pain with his heart attacks and this felt much more like his stomach. Then he was sick and after that he felt a little better. I gave him some medicine for his stomach from the medical kit and then I checked on my first patient and he said he felt a lot better.

> *If you're a doctor, your first instinct is to hide in the toilet.*

A couple of hours later, a flight attendant woke me from a deep sleep (this was an overnight flight) to apologetically tell me that there was a third passenger in need of attention. This time it was an elderly lady who was having trouble breathing and the flight attendants had got an oxygen mask on her. Well, her lungs were clear and her pulse was normal and she seemed really panicky, and her travelling companion said she had been under a lot of stress and hated flying. So this was probably a panic attack. I told the flight attendant to keep her on oxygen for another half an hour and told the patient in my most reassuring tone that she would be feeling better soon. I then checked on the kidney stone patient (sleeping) and the sick man (much better, thank you). I went back to the galley and had some coffee with the crew, then went back to the panicky lady, who was feeling much better.

The flight crew was very nice and gave me a free bottle of champagne as a gift. But when we landed I decided I would never again admit that I was a doctor on an aircraft flight!

Glossary

a kidney stone a painful medical condition
elderly old
abdominal pain stomach pain
to be sick to bring food back from the stomach
lungs the organs in your body which you use to breathe

In-flight emergencies

Taking charge in an emergency

SPEAKING

1 Emergencies are all about *Safety first*, the most important part of the flight attendant's training. In an on-board emergency, which of these roles does the flight attendant take: diplomat, nurse, policeman, firefighter, referee, lifesaver? Discuss with a partner or in small groups. Which is the most important role?

2 Work with a partner. Look at the list of serious on-board events. Which are real emergencies? Which are the most serious? Which are the least serious? Can you add any more to the list?

  a an engine on fire
  b a passenger giving birth
  c passengers fighting
  d a sudden loss of cabin pressure and drop in altitude
  e complete engine failure
  f a PAN-PAN call as a result of a cardiac arrest
  g a fire in the toilets
  h lots of passengers suffering from nausea
  i the pilot's PA announcement to prepare for ditching
  j an aborted take-off (or go-around)

As you discuss the situations, think about these questions.

➤ Which is life-threatening to all on board?
➤ Which is a temporary problem?
➤ Which is a clear Mayday?
➤ Which is a PAN-PAN?

3 Which of these things would you do in an emergency situation?

  a Discuss the situation with your colleagues.
  b Wait for instructions from the purser.
  c Ask the passengers for their advice.
  d Give clear instructions to passengers on what to do.

LISTENING

 AUDIO 7.1

4 Try to fill in the missing words in this sudden announcement from the purser. Then listen and check your answers.

Purser Ladies and gentlemen, this is an ¹_____. This is an ²_____.
³_____ in your seats with your seatbelts ⁴_____. Remain ⁵_____ and ⁶_____ these instructions. Pull ⁷_____ the oxygen mask. Pull ⁸_____ the oxygen mask. Put it ⁹_____ your nose and ¹⁰_____ immediately and breathe ¹¹_____.

Flight attendant Grab your mask. Pull it down and place it ¹²_____ your nose and ¹³_____.

Purser Remain calm. Stay in your seats and ¹⁴_____ a mask towards you. Place the mask over your mouth and nose like this and breathe normally, adjusting the ¹⁵_____ to secure it. Do make sure your own mask is fitted properly ¹⁶_____ helping anyone else.

LANGUAGE FOCUS

GIVING INSTRUCTIONS

Study these instructions.

Stay in your seats.
Remain calm.
Pull down the oxygen mask.
Pull it down over your nose and mouth.
Breathe normally.

 PRONUNCIATION

 AUDIO 7.2

5 Listen and repeat the instructions in *Language focus*.

 SPEAKING

6 In all emergencies, cabin crew must give clear instructions, calm the passengers and act quickly. Work with a partner. During an emergency situation, what would you say to these people? Choose from the sentences below. There may be several possible answers.

a a worried passenger whose wife has just fainted
b a pregnant woman experiencing contractions
c a young boy running in the aisle to the toilet
d a panicky hyper-ventilating passenger
e a loud and noisy group who are not taking the emergency instructions seriously
f a mother whose child is sick and vomiting
g a woman with headphones who is listening to music

➤ Please keep quiet.
➤ Don't worry, you'll be fine.
➤ Listen, stop.
➤ Don't be upset. We'll take care of her.
➤ Keep quiet please – you are disturbing others.
➤ Don't shout, speak normally.
➤ Breathe slowly and deeply. That's it.
➤ Calm down now, please.
➤ That's enough – control yourself.
➤ Try to relax. I'll stay with you.
➤ Listen carefully, please, these instructions are for you.
➤ Wait until we land.

Preparing for an emergency evacuation

READING

1 **Read about this emergency. Have you ever been in a situation like this? If so, what happened? Tell a partner.**

Flight JWZ157 is in trouble. It is a Boeing 747 with 174 passengers and 14 crew. After experiencing severe turbulence and the start of a fire in one engine, the captain has decided to shut down the engine and make an emergency landing. The captain makes the announcement himself. The passengers are aware that all is not normal and they are nervous.

LISTENING

AUDIO 7.3

2 **Listen to the captain's announcement to the passengers and fill in the missing words.**

Ladies and gentlemen, your captain ¹_____. We have a ²_____ problem and for everyone's safety we've decided to land in the next ³_____ minutes at the nearest airport. The landing should be perfectly ⁴_____, but for safety reasons we will evacuate the aircraft using the ⁵_____. The cabin crew will now give you full instructions and ⁶_____ you for the landing. Please listen ⁷_____ to their instructions. Thank you.

SPEAKING

3 **What do you think will happen after the captain's announcement? What won't happen? Put a tick (✓) or a cross (✗).**

The cabin crew will ...

a secure everything in the galleys
b continue the food and drinks service
c help passengers to get their bags from the lockers to collect precious items
d begin to go through the cabin saying 'fasten seatbelts'
e make sure the toilets are empty
f collect the headsets
g make sure everyone returns to their seats immediately
h wait for instructions
i point out the emergency exits.

LISTENING

AUDIO 7.4

4 **Listen to the purser giving further instructions to the passengers and fill in the missing words.**

a Ladies and gentlemen, as the captain has just told you, we shall be landing in 20 minutes. For safety reasons, after landing we shall be ¹_____ the aircraft using the ²_____ slides. So please listen very carefully and do ³_____ as instructed. Please return to your seats immediately and ⁴_____ your seatbelt fastened securely.

(Later)

b We are now ⁵_____ to take you through our safety procedures. Please watch and listen carefully. The safety card in your seat pocket ⁶_____ details of your escape routes, oxygen masks and life jackets. It also shows the ⁷_____ position, which you must adopt in an emergency landing. Again, please listen carefully.

Emergency exits are on both ⁸_____ of the aircraft. They are clearly ⁹_____ and are being ¹⁰_____ out to you now. On the main deck there are two exits at the rear of the First class cabin and two at the front and rear of each other cabin section. On the upper deck there is an emergency exit on each side, in the middle of the cabin.

Please take a moment now to ¹¹_____ the exit nearest to you, bearing in mind that the nearest usable exit may be behind you. To help you find your way to the exits, ¹²_____ lighting is provided in the aisles at floor level.

(After landing)

c Please remain seated and follow instructions given to you by your crew. Do not leave your seats until instructed to do so by your crew. When the seatbelt signs are switched off, make your way to your nearest exit. Leave all personal ¹³_____ behind. I repeat, leave all personal hand-baggage ¹⁴_____. Ladies, ¹⁵_____ high-heeled shoes, as they may tear the slide.

LANGUAGE FOCUS

Study these sentences.

INSTRUCTIONS
NOT TO DO
SOMETHING

Do not leave your seats until instructed to do so by your crew.
Do not / Don't take anything with you as you leave the aircraft.
Do not / Don't take handbags or briefcases.

SPEAKING

5 **In groups of three, practise speaking the three parts of the announcement made by the purser. Then say them again from memory or short notes.**

Reporting an evacuation

Airline accidents are very rare and fatal accidents even more so. In 2010 the Polish president and many top public figures died when their jet crashed en route to a war memorial service in Russia. This was one of the most notable crashes in recent time, along with the Concorde crash in 2000 in Paris. In both these incidents there were no survivors and there is nothing that the cabin crew could have done to avert disaster. Cabin crew were, however, able to play an important part in an incident involving US Airways flight 1549 in February 2009. You are going to read a newspaper article about this incident.

1 Look at the photograph below. Describe what you can see in the picture.

2 Read the headline. What do you know about this incident?

UNBELIEVABLE

BUT TRUE

US Airways Flight 1549 lost both engines following a massive bird-strike three and a half minutes after take-off and made an emergency landing in the Hudson River yesterday in the late afternoon. There were 150 passengers and five crew members, including the captain, first officer and three flight attendants, on board. All 155 survived.

The plane ditched at exactly 15.31, less than seven minutes after take-off. Four minutes later all the passengers and crew had been evacuated on to the wings of the floating aircraft or into the slightly submerged slides. They were then taken to safety on Hudson River ferries. Before leaving the aircraft himself, the captain made one last check inside to see that no one was left behind. There were no serious injuries.

Many are calling this a miracle. However, aviation authorities are saying that the real reason for the success of the landing and evacuation was the first-class training of the pilots and cabin crew. They knew what to do and did it superbly.

3 This incident has been described as the most successful ditching in aviation history. Do you agree? What do you know about the actions of the cabin crew and flight crew that day?

READING

4 **Read the newspaper report and answer the questions.**

1 What caused the engine failure?
2 Where did the plane land? On water or on land?
3 How many people were injured?
4 Who was the last person to leave the aircraft?
5 What reason do aviation authorities give for the 'miracle'?

VOCABULARY

5 **Match words from the newspaper report with these definitions.**

1 very big _____
2 an attack _____
3 to live after a bad accident _____
4 to land a plane on water _____
5 not sinking under the water _____
6 just a little _____
7 under water _____
8 physical harm _____
9 very, very good _____
10 very well _____

LANGUAGE FOCUS

REPORTING INSTRUCTIONS

Study these sentences.

Captain to crew: 'Prepare the cabin for an emergency landing.'	The captain **told** the crew **to** prepare the cabin for an emergency landing.
Flight attendant to passengers: 'Take off your shoes.'	The flight attendant **told** the passengers **to** take off their shoes.
Flight attendant to passengers: 'Don't get anything from the overhead lockers.'	The flight attendant **told** the passengers **not to** get anything from the overhead lockers.
Purser to passengers: 'Don't worry.'	The purser **told** the passengers **not to** worry.

PRONUNCIATION

 AUDIO 7.5

6 **Listen to these sentences and notice how the weak _to_ /tə/ is not stressed.**

➤ The captain told the crew **to** prepare the cabin for an emergency landing.
➤ The flight attendant told the passengers **to** take off their shoes.
➤ The flight attendant told the passengers not **to** get anything from the overhead lockers.
➤ The purser told the passengers not **to** worry.

Now listen again and repeat the sentences.

SPEAKING

7 **Work with a partner. Imagine what happened inside the aircraft in the Hudson River incident and take turns to tell the story, using questions and answers. Give and get as much detail as possible. Talk about the instructions that were given and all the things the crew and passengers had to do.**

Some questions from the reporter might be: *What happened? What did you do? How did the passengers / crew react? Then what happened?*

Situation 1: Student A is a TV reporter; Student B is a crew member.
Situation 2: Student A is a passenger; Student B is a TV reporter.

Case study

READING

1 Read *Crew's response to take-off incident criticized* opposite and answer the questions.

1 Put these events from the incident into the correct order.

a _____ Conditions in the cabin got worse.
b _____ The flight crew heard a bump.
c _____ The aircraft landed safely.
d _____ The passenger oxygen system was deployed manually.
e _____ A passenger received medical assistance.
f _____ Nine oxygen masks failed to deploy.
g _____ The flight crew continued climbing and pressurizing the cabin.
h _____ The cabin supervisor banged on the cockpit door.

2 How did the flight attendants try to help when some of the oxygen masks did not deploy?

SPEAKING

2 Work with a partner. Answer the questions and discuss the emergency in the text.

1 What kind of training do flight attendants get for such emergencies?
2 Would you have done things differently if you had been on this flight? What would you have said to the passengers and the other crew members? Who is responsible for talking to the captain?

LISTENING

  AUDIO 7.6

3 Listen to Shon Davis as she answers these questions. Make notes about what she says.

1 'What was the most serious emergency you experienced?'
2 'Did you ever have to evacuate passengers?'
3 'What special qualities as a flight attendant do you need in emergencies?'

4 Listen again and answer the questions.

1 Describe the Lusaka experience. What does Shon say about these things?
  ➤ V1
  ➤ braking
  ➤ her senior crew member
  ➤ people in the Business class section
  ➤ communication from the flight deck

2 Tell a partner the story of the evacuation. What does Shon say about these things?
  ➤ the announcements from the captain   ➤ the fuel tanks
  ➤ the tyres on the aircraft   ➤ passengers behaving selfishly

3 Complete what Shon says about dealing with an emergency. Do you agree with her analysis?
  'I think all flight attendants have to be able to ¹_____ with pressure and ²_____.
  They have to be able to demonstrate a calmness and they have to also be ³_____ and feel
  confident about what they are doing and what their role is, and what their responsibility as a
  safety officer on board is, and if you can be ⁴_____, if you can absorb your training and
  know your ⁵_____ as to what to do in any given situation, particularly emergency, then the
  training will automatically take over and your calm ⁶_____ plus your training will help you
  deal with the situation in the best way possible.'

SPEAKING

5 Work with a partner. Discuss these questions.

1 Are you surprised by how the flight attendants reacted during and after the Lusaka evacuation?
2 In emergencies, do you wait for orders or follow your training and act quickly? Do you think your training prepares you for emergency incidents?
3 What was your worst experience of an emergency, either as a flight attendant or as a passenger?

Crew's response to take-off incident criticized

Nine oxygen masks failed to deploy and cabin crew had to bang on the cockpit door to alert the pilot during a serious incident on a flight from Dublin to London, according to an air accident investigation.

Six crew and 148 passengers were on the flight to London Stansted. At take-off, the flight crew heard a bump, but were not sure what had happened. The tail of the aircraft had hit the runway during take-off, but it was four minutes before the cabin crew could confirm that a tail-strike had occurred. During this time the flight crew decided to continue climbing and pressurizing the cabin, even though the nature of the problem was not known.

As part of the standard procedures after such an event, the flight crew opened the pressurization outflow valve and this caused the cabin to depressurize quickly. Environmental conditions in the cabin then rapidly deteriorated, and the cabin supervisor tried unsuccessfully to speak to the flight crew on the intercom.

When the supervisor failed to reach the captain by phone, she banged on the cockpit door and established communication. 'I ran to the front. I needed to inform the captain that we were having a rapid recompression.'

After this, the passenger oxygen system was deployed manually, but some masks did not deploy. 'The passengers in the row in front of me did not have masks on and were striking the overhead lockers with their hands to try and get them to open,' one passenger told the investigation. Cabin crew helped them to move to spare seats where the masks had deployed, and even used their ID cards in an effort to open the units where oxygen masks were stored.

The aircraft landed safely after 21 minutes in the air and one passenger received medical assistance. The investigation report said that while the tail-strike was not serious, what followed caused a serious incident which upset many passengers.

The airline, which has accepted what the report says, has already made changes to its training procedures in response to the incident. It said the report showed that the tail-strike was minor, and that the aircraft returned to Dublin as a precaution.

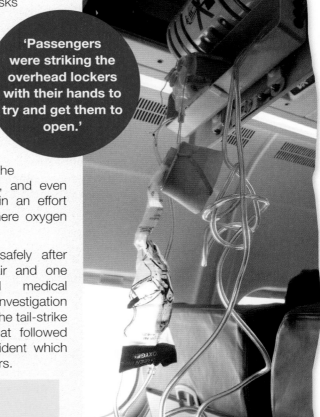

> **'Passengers were striking the overhead lockers with their hands to try and get them to open.'**

Glossary

to deploy to use; to come into use
tail-strike when the aircraft tail hits the ground on take-off
pressurization outflow valve something that regulates the amount of air needed to be released from the cabin in order to maintain the required amount of pressurization
to deteriorate to get worse
rapid very fast
manually by hand; not automatically
a precaution a safety measure

Complaints and disruptive passengers

Responding to passenger complaints

SPEAKING

1 Some passengers will complain about everything! Work with a partner. Look at the list of things people sometimes complain about. Which do you think are the most common? Can you think of any more things to add?

> flight delays and waiting time
> the service
> the food
> the cabin temperature
> the seating arrangements
> the drinks
> the lack of information
> the state of the toilets
> ... even the cabin crew!

2 With your partner, discuss what people say when they complain about the things in exercise 1.

LISTENING

3 As the flight attendant, you must respond positively to complaints. First, look at three complaints during the meals service. What would you say in reply to these passengers?

1 Excuse me, we've been waiting for drinks for a long time. We finished eating 20 minutes ago.
2 I'm sorry, I can't eat this meal – it's cold!
3 This is not what I asked for. I ordered a vegetarian meal!

 AUDIO 8.1

4 Now listen to the flight attendants' replies and complete the sentences.

1 Oh, I do understand. I _____. It's been so _____. What can I _____ you?
2 Oh dear, that's not _____. I'm _____ sorry. Let me take it _____ for you and see if I can get you a hot cooked meal immediately.
3 Oh, _____. I'm sorry about this. Please, be _____. Let me just check the _____ meals list.

SPEAKING

5 **The flight attendant must be a *diplomat*. It is important to sympathize, apologize, give a good reason where possible, and then find a solution. Look at the first reply again and see how it follows this pattern:**

1 Sympathize: *I do understand.*
Apologize: *I apologize.*
Give a reason: *It's been so busy.*
Find a solution: *What can I get you?*

Analyse the other two replies in the same way.

2 Sympathize: _____
Apologize: _____
Find a solution: _____

3 Sympathize: _____
Apologize: _____
Find a solution: _____

Is it always a good idea to give a reason or excuse for a problem? Are there times when it is better not to give excuses?

LANGUAGE FOCUS

OFFERING TO HELP (2)

Study these sentences.

Let me just check the special meals list.
Let me get an official form for you.
Let me see if I can get you another one.
Let me get you a blanket.

PRONUNCIATION

 AUDIO 8.2

6 **Listen and repeat the sentences in *Language focus*.**

LISTENING

 AUDIO 8.3

7 **Listen to five complaints and identify each problem. Decide what you would say in response.**

1 _____
_____
2 _____
_____
3 _____
_____
4 _____
_____
5 _____
_____

 AUDIO 8.4

8 **Now listen to the responses of the flight attendants to the five complaints. How well do you think they dealt with the complaints?**

9 **Fill in the missing words in some of the key expressions used by the flight attendants when dealing with the problems in exercise 8. Listen again if you need to.**

1 Thank you for _____ me know, and I do _____.
2 I do apologize, sir. I know how _____ it is.
3 I'm sorry _____ that.
4 I'm _____ that you haven't _____ your flight.
5 We've had _____ many problems today and I can _____ apologize.

Dealing with complaints about other passengers

1 What sort of complaints can passengers make about other passengers? In your experience, which are the most common?

What do you do when passengers complain about other passengers?

 AUDIO 8.5

2 Listen to a passenger complaining to a flight attendant, Josef, and answer the questions.

1 Why is the passenger angry?
2 What does the passenger want to do?
3 What does the flight attendant, Josef, suggest?
4 Is the passenger satisfied?

What do you think happens next?

3 Listen again to the conversation and fill in the missing words.

Passenger 1 Excuse me, listen, I can't sit here any longer. That group of people is making too much noise. They are ¹_____ me and everyone around. If you can't do anything about it, you'll have to find me another seat. I ²_____ to sit here any longer.

Josef Hmm, yes, I ³_____. I can hear how noisy they are and I'm sorry they are disturbing you. Have you spoken to them yourself?

Passenger 1 Of course not. I don't think they ⁴_____ about me or anyone else.

Josef Let me have a ⁵_____ with them. If it doesn't get better, then I'll try to find you another seat, although the plane is pretty full. ⁶_____ about that?

Passenger 1 Well, er ... yes, OK. Thank you. That would be fine.

 AUDIO 8.6 **4** Listen to Josef describing the problem to his colleague, Hans. Answer the questions.

1 Will be it possible to move the angry passenger?
2 What will Josef have to do to deal with the situation?
3 What will Hans do to help?

AUDIO 8.7 **5** **Josef is talking to the group of noisy passengers. Try to fill in the missing words, then listen and check your answers.**

Josef	Excuse me, excuse me. Listen guys, are you ¹_____ the flight?
Passenger 2	Yes, yes, sure.
Passenger 3	You bet, it's great.
Josef	²_____. Could I ask you a special ³_____? Would you mind just keeping your voices ⁴_____ a little? You're getting a little loud and some people are ⁵_____ to sleep or watch a film.
Passenger 2	Why? Who's complaining?
Passenger 3	Are we making a lot of ⁶_____?
Josef	No-one's complained, but we can ⁷_____ you all in the galley!
Passenger 2	Oh, OK, no problem.
Passenger 3	OK.
Passenger 2	How about ⁸_____ drink?
Josef	Sure, I'll get you another drink if you keep your voices down. Thanks for your ⁹_____.

6 **How well do you think Josef dealt with the situation? Is there anything you would handle differently?**

LANGUAGE FOCUS

IF ...

Study these sentences.

If the situation doesn't get better, then I'll try to find you another seat.
If there's still a problem, then I'll come over.
If there is still a problem, I won't leave you on your own.
I'll get you another drink if you keep your voices down.

PRONUNCIATION

AUDIO 8.8

7 **Listen and repeat the sentences in *Language focus*.**

AUDIO 8.9 **8** **Listen and repeat these requests to passengers and crew from the flight attendant. Notice the very polite intonation.**

➤ Could I ask you a special favour?
➤ Would you mind just keeping the noise down a little?
➤ Please could you come over to help me?

SPEAKING **9** **Work in pairs or groups of three. Role-play a situation like the one in exercise 5. Use your own ideas and follow this format.**

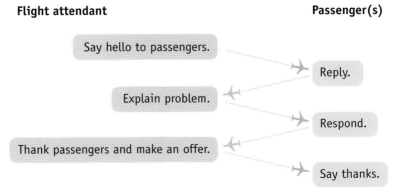

Flight attendant

Say hello to passengers.

Explain problem.

Thank passengers and make an offer.

Passenger(s)

Reply.

Respond.

Say thanks.

Now swap roles and role-play the situation again. Who dealt with the problem best?

Managing disruptive passengers

1 Sometimes difficult situations with passengers get out of control. Passengers become aggressive, insulting or drunk and refuse to do what they are asked.

Work with a partner. What are your procedures for dealing with really disruptive passengers? What can you do in situations a–c below? What can't you do?

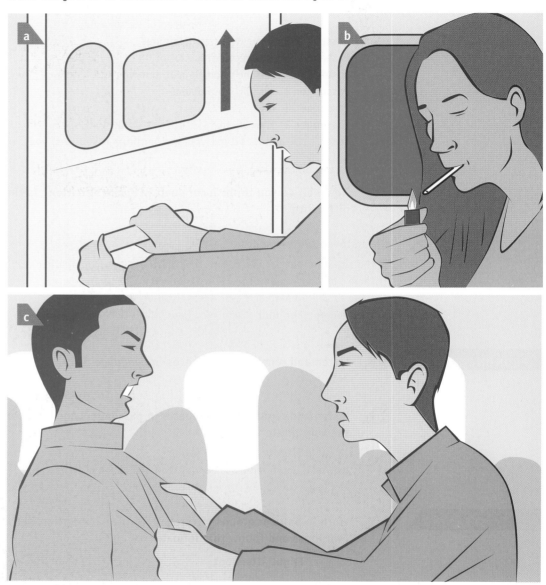

 AUDIO 8.10

2 Listen to flight attendants Jenny and Tom and purser Ted dealing with a very disruptive passenger. Answer the questions.

1 What is the problem with the passenger?
2 What does the passenger want?
3 How does Jenny describe the passenger to Tom?
4 What does the passenger say he is going to do?
5 How do the flight attendants deal with the situation?
6 What does Ted say he has to do?
7 What does Ted say they will need after landing?
8 What does Ted tell Tom to do with the other passengers?

3 **Complete this report on the incident.**

About half an hour before ¹_____, a drunk passenger became ²_____ because he was refused more ³_____. He began to ⁴_____ and scream and it took ⁵_____ cabin crew members and other passengers to ⁶_____ him. His wrists were eventually ⁷_____ to a seat by the ⁸_____, but he did not ⁹_____ down. The captain was informed and the local ¹⁰_____ met the plane on arrival and arrested the passenger.

LANGUAGE FOCUS

EXPRESSING
OBLIGATION

Study these sentences.

I have to speak to the captain.
I've got to speak to the captain.
I must speak to the captain.

We must call the police / security.
We need to call the police / security.

PRONUNCIATION

 AUDIO 8.11

4 **Listen and repeat these sentences expressing obligation. Notice the pronunciation of *have to*.**

➤ You have to sit down, sir.
➤ I have to speak to the captain.
➤ You have to stop that now.
➤ You have to be quiet.
➤ You have to do what the captain says.

 AUDIO 8.12

5 **Now listen and practise these sentences you can use for dealing with passengers affected by the incident.**

➤ Would you come to the back of the plane with me, please, madam?
➤ I can see how upset you are.
➤ Can you tell me exactly what happened?
➤ I do apologize. Incidents like this are extremely rare.
➤ Please don't worry.
➤ Everything is under control.

Case study

READING **1** **Read the newspaper articles opposite and answer the questions.**

1 Make a list of the different kinds of unruly and disruptive behaviour mentioned in the articles. Put them in order of seriousness from 1 to 5, where 5 = extremely serious.

2 What seems to be the main cause of the bad behaviour you read about? Or are there several reasons for it?

SPEAKING **2** **Work with a partner. Discuss the questions about disruptive passengers.**

1 Discuss the reactions of the cabin crew where they are mentioned in the articles. Do you think that flight attendants are given enough training to deal with unruly passengers?

2 Why is the problem of 'air rage' growing? What can be done to prevent or limit it? For example, do you think alcohol should be banned on flights?

3 How is airline security and the safety of all on board at risk from disruptive passengers?

LISTENING **3** **Listen to Shon Davis as she answers these questions. Make notes about what she says.**

 AUDIO 8.13

1 'Why are difficult passengers the flight attendant's biggest headache?'

2 'What was the worst experience you had?'

3 'How do you deal with such difficult passengers?'

4 **Listen again and answer the questions.**

1 Why does Shon say difficult passengers are 'frustrating'? What did she always try to do?

2 Work with a partner. Tell the story of Shon's worst experience in your own words. What did the passenger complain about? How did Shon succeed in changing the passenger's attitude? What did he say as he left the plane?

3 Why did the man want to move to Business class? What alternative did Shon find for him? Was he happy with this solution?

SPEAKING **5** **Work with a partner. Discuss these questions.**

1 What is the difference between difficult passengers and disruptive passengers?

2 What is your airline's policy on air rage incidents?

3 What is the best way to deal with really disruptive passengers? Does airline policy take different cultures and customs into consideration?

Incidents of unruly and disruptive behaviour by passengers on board aircraft appear to be increasing in frequency and severity on flights. It is sometimes referred to as 'air rage'. It can also be defined as any behaviour on board an aircraft which interferes with the crew in the conduct of their duties and disrupts the safe operation of an aircraft. Here are some recent examples.

FIGHTING PASSENGERS CAUSE PLANE TO DIVERT

A brawl between rival football fans forced a plane to make an emergency landing in Germany last Friday. The men, aged 24 and 36, had been drinking and could not be restrained by cabin crew after they started fighting.

Vegas flight lands in Denver after air rage incident

A US airliner en route to Las Vegas was diverted to Denver after a passenger tried to open an exterior door on the plane, officials say. The man had reportedly consumed alcohol before and during the flight. 'There was a disturbance on board involving an unruly passenger, and the pilots decided to divert to Denver,' local police said in a statement.

ABUSIVE FLYER OFFLOADED FROM AIRCRAFT

An aircraft returned to its parking bay after taxiing for take-off to offload a passenger who had become abusive with a cabin crew member. 'The cabin crew member asked him to put his seat upright, but received verbal abuse in response,' said an airline official. It is not known whether the passenger was drunk. When informed of the incident, the captain decided to turn the aircraft back to the parking bay to offload the unruly passenger.

Woman who hit attendants jailed after forced landing of Tokyo flight

A 42-year-old woman has been jailed after causing a trans-Pacific flight to be diverted to Anchorage, Alaska.

The woman was aboard the Delta Airlines flight from Tokyo to New York when, about 45 minutes into the flight, she began assaulting a flight attendant who was offering a beverage service. Flight attendants tried to calm her, but she continued screaming profanities in Japanese and hit four flight attendants before being handcuffed and seat-belted in her seat. She continued to struggle and unbuckled her seatbelt several times, causing flight attendants to set up a 30-minute rotation to watch her. Pilots were forced to dump 70,000 pounds of jet fuel to land in Anchorage and hand her over to local police.

Drunk passenger jailed after going on rampage at 30,000ft

A drunken airline passenger went on a rampage at 30,000 feet after cabin crew caught him trying to get into the first-class section. During the nine-and-a-half hour flight, the man, who was travelling in Economy class, walked up and down the aisles shouting abuse, reducing passengers to tears and causing his own daughter, aged 15, to go and sit with the crew to hide from him. He was jailed for eight months after pleading guilty to being drunk on an aircraft.

One too many

A passenger was arrested on Friday after his flight landed on charges that he assaulted and intimidated the flight crew. The man drank five glasses of wine after boarding the flight in Atlanta, Georgia, authorities said. He became abusive when flight attendants refused to serve him a sixth drink. When the senior flight attendant arrived to try to calm him, he grabbed her arms and hands. Flight attendants armed themselves with a fire extinguisher and positioned drinks trolleys in the aisles in case the man tried to get into the cockpit.

Glossary

a brawl a fight
a forced landing an unscheduled landing
profanities abusive language
to dump to throw away
to go on a rampage to go around causing damage
to set up a rotation to take turns in a continuous task

Preparing for landing

Making final announcements and checks

SPEAKING

1 **Work with a partner. What do you usually do at stages a–c below?**

a 20 minutes before landing
b 10 minutes before landing
c 2 minutes before landing

2 **What are the difficulties for cabin crew at the end of the flight? How do you usually feel then? Stressed? Tired? Happy because the flight will soon be over?**

LISTENING

 AUDIO 9.1

3 **Before or during the descent, the captain usually informs passengers of the local time and temperature at the destination airport, and the time remaining until arrival. This is followed by a further announcement from one of the cabin crew. Listen to this second announcement. What three things do the flight attendants have to do?**

4 **Try to complete the purser's announcement you heard. Then listen again and check your answers.**

Ladies and gentlemen, we'll ¹_____ be landing at Montreal Trudeau Airport. The 'Fasten seatbelts' signs have been ²_____ on. Please return to your seat and ³_____ your hand-baggage is safely secured in the overhead lockers or ⁴_____ the seat in front of you. Please also make sure your table is folded ⁵_____, your seat back is upright, with the arm-rest ⁶_____ and your seatbelt is fastened.

Passengers seated in our First and Business class cabins, please make sure that your foot-rest and video screens are back in their original ⁷_____.

If you have been using the in-seat ⁸_____, we will shortly be switching it off, so please now unplug your laptop and store it in a safe place.

Once again, may we remind you that cell phones ⁹_____ not be switched on until the seatbelt signs have been switched off after landing.

We hope that you've enjoyed the in-flight entertainment during the flight. In preparation for landing we'll be switching the system off. It would greatly ¹⁰_____ the flight attendants if you could have your used headsets ¹¹_____ for collection as they pass through the cabin.

PRONUNCIATION

 AUDIO 9.2

5 **Listen again to these parts of the purser's announcement and practise saying them.**

1 Please return to your seat and ensure your hand-baggage is safely secured in the overhead lockers or under the seat in front of you.
2 Please make sure that your foot-rest and video screens are back in their original position.
3 If you have been using the in-seat power, we will shortly be switching it off, so please now unplug your laptop and store it in a safe place.
4 May we remind you that cell phones must not be switched on until the seatbelt signs have been switched off after landing.

SPEAKING | **6** | Work with a partner. Practise making the purser's announcement. First, read it aloud. Then say it again from memory or notes.

LISTENING
AUDIO 9.3

7 The cabin crew are passing through the cabin. Listen to the flight attendant speaking to three passengers and complete the sentences.

1 Can you open the window _____, please?
2 I can't find my _____ form.
3 I'll bring you _____ in a few minutes.
4 Put your bags under the seat in _____, please.
5 Ah, this is an _____ row, so _____ has to go in the overhead lockers, please.
6 Sorry to _____ you.
7 Do you know how long it _____ to get from the airport to the city?
8 We take the company _____.
9 _____ says the train is the fastest.
10 And, sorry, could you take your _____ off the empty seat and put it in the _____, please?

LANGUAGE FOCUS | Study these sentences.

WORD ORDER
IN MULTI-WORD
VERBS

Put away the case.   Put it away.
Turn / Switch off your electronic devices.   Turn / Switch them off.
Fold away your table.   Fold it away.
Turn up / down the heating.   Turn it up / down.

Put your seat back upright.   Put it upright.
Put your bags in the locker.   Put them in the locker.

SPEAKING | **8** | Work with a partner. Practise asking passengers to do things in preparation for landing. Use this illustration.

Giving information about delayed landings

1 Passengers often get upset when landing is delayed. Work with a partner. Look at the reasons for delayed landings in the picture. Can you think of any more? Practise explaining them to passengers.

 AUDIO 9.4

2 The first officer has already announced the landing and begun the descent. Listen to the conversation between a flight attendant and a passenger. Answer the questions.

1 What has the passenger noticed?
2 What is the passenger worried about?
3 What possible reason does the flight attendant give for the delay?
4 What does the flight attendant suggest?

3 **Listen to the first officer's second announcement, and the second conversation between the flight attendant and the passenger. Answer the questions.**

1 How long will the delay be?
2 What is the reason given for the delay?
3 What time does the flight attendant expect the flight to land?
4 What time is the passenger's connecting flight?
5 What does the passenger have to do in Paris?
6 What is it not necessary for the passenger to do in Paris?

How well do you think the flight attendant deals with the situation? Would you do anything differently? What do you say when you have to deal with a situation where you have no control?

LANGUAGE FOCUS

TALKING ABOUT TIME

Study these sentences.

What time / When does the flight land / take off?
It lands / takes off at 10.15.
What time / When is the flight?
At 10.15.
How long does it take to get / go to the domestic terminal?
It takes about five minutes.
How long is the flight?
About two hours.

READING

4 **Read these two further announcements from the flight deck. What is the specific reason for the delay? What happens in the end?**

First officer Ladies and gentlemen, your first officer again with more news of our delay. The reason for the delay is that there is only one runway in operation due to an earlier incident on the ground. Air Traffic Control have warned us of a possible longer delay. Please remain seated with your seatbelts on in case we are given the all clear to land. I will get back to you as soon as we have more news.

Captain Ladies and gentlemen, this is your captain speaking. Matters are not improving on the ground and we shall be diverting to Bordeaux. We expect to land there in 35 minutes. I understand that this may cause inconvenience, but it is the quickest and safest option.
Our ground staff will meet you on arrival and help you with your onward journey. If you have a serious problem, kindly advise the cabin crew, who will be going through the cabin shortly. Again, my apologies for this inconvenience and thank you for your cooperation.

SPEAKING

5 **Work with a partner. Take turns to practise dealing with a passenger who has to make a connection when the landing is delayed.**

Passenger   **Flight attendant**

State your problem.

Sympathize and ask for more information.

Demand a solution to your problem.

Do your best to find a solution to the problem.

Getting through the final ten minutes

'Cabin crew, ten minutes to landing, ten minutes to landing.

SPEAKING

1 What does this call from the flight deck mean for the cabin crew? What does it mean for passengers? What happens next?

LISTENING

 AUDIO 9.6

2 Listen to Leila talking to Tom, Jutta and Hemal in the moments before landing and answer the questions.

1 Has Tom checked his side of the cabin?
2 What does Leila ask Tom to do?
3 What hasn't Jutta done yet?
4 Why isn't Tom's side of the cabin secure yet?
5 What does Leila tell Tom to do about the passenger in the toilet?
6 Does Jutta manage to complete her paperwork in time before landing?

VOCABULARY

3 Complete these phrases and sentences from the Listening with the correct preposition.

1 paperwork _____ customs
2 clear _____ the cabin
3 help _____ the C209s
4 Cabin crew, seats _____ landing.
5 bang _____ the door
6 Get him _____ his seat fast.

LANGUAGE FOCUS

**CHECKING THINGS
HAVE BEEN DONE**

Study these sentences.

Have you done all the checks?
Yes, I've completed all the checks.
Yes, I have.
Have you done all the clearing in?
No, I haven't cleared in all the rows (yet).
No, I haven't.
Has she finished the bar paperwork?
Yes, she has. / No, she hasn't.

PRONUNCIATION

 AUDIO 9.7

4 **Listen and repeat these questions and answers. Notice the way the intonation goes up in the question and down in the short answers.**

Has she done the final checks?	No, she hasn't.
Have you secured the trolley in the galley?	Yes, I have.
Have they checked the tables are upright?	No, they haven't.
Have we done everything?	Yes, we have.

5 **Work with a partner. Which of these sentences would the crew use during the last 20 minutes of the flight, and which during the last ten minutes?**

1 Have you filled in your disembarkation card, sir?
2 Any rubbish?
3 I'm sorry, you'll have to wait until we land now, sir.
4 Could you put your seat upright, please, sir?
5 Could you remove your headset, please, madam?
6 I'm afraid the toilet is now locked for landing, madam.
7 This is the emergency exit door, sir. You'll have to put your bag in the overhead locker.
8 I'm sorry, it's too late now, madam.
9 Please, sir, I've asked you before, you must switch off your laptop immediately.
10 Could you fasten your child's seatbelt, please, sir?
11 Could you just open the window blind? Thanks.
12 Yes, but not now – I'll tell you after landing.

SPEAKING

6 **It is less than five minutes to landing. In pairs, practise asking and answering questions about final checks. One of you is a senior flight attendant, the other a junior flight attendant.**

When you have completed the conversation, reverse roles and do it again.

Case study

READING Read *Toilet troubles for Cathay* opposite and answer the questions.

1 What was the special problem on the Hong Kong flight?
2 What were the consequences for everyone involved?
3 What do you think the cabin crew had to do?

SPEAKING Work with a partner. Discuss these questions.

1 Have you experienced similar problems with toilets on flights? If so, what did you tell the passengers?
2 What guidelines for toilet management during flights are you given? Are they adequate?
3 Write an announcement about a blocked toilet and practise giving it to passengers. Use these phrases to help you.

> out of order ■ experiencing a problem ■ to the front / middle / rear of the aircraft
> until further notice ■ toilet facilities ■ apologize for any inconvenience

LISTENING Listen to Shon Davis as she answers these questions. Make notes about what she says.

 AUDIO 9.8

1 'Is preparing for landing easier than preparing for take-off?'
2 'Do you remember any special problems with passengers in the final ten minutes?'
3 'Can you briefly outline communications in the final phases of descent?'

Listen again and answer the questions.

1 Before landing, what has to be collected, checked, handed out, secured and stowed by the flight attendants?
2 Why exactly did the 'foreign lady' cause 'a bit of a panic'? How can this kind of situation be avoided? What should have happened?
3 What does Shon say about communication between ...
➤ pilot / co-pilot and passengers?
➤ passengers and cabin crew?
➤ flight crew and cabin crew?

SPEAKING Work with a partner. Discuss these questions.

1 Do you agree that preparing for landing is the most stressful part of the flight? If so, why?
2 On long-haul flights, why doesn't the captain announce the beginning of the descent at least 30 minutes before landing, to give cabin crew more time to perform all their duties? On short-haul flights, is 20 minutes enough for the cabin crew?
3 Can you suggest improvements to the communications between the flight crew and the cabin crew, and among the cabin crew, during the last ten minutes before landing? What is standard practice on your airline?
4 How do you deal with passengers who ask for information about baggage, transit, how to get into town, and so on when you are preparing for landing?
5 Is there any difference in the preparation for landing between long-haul and short-haul flights?

TOILET TROUBLES FOR CATHAY

Toilets on planes, especially on long-haul flights, are often the subject of complaints by the travelling public. They say they are often dirty, uncared for, not cleaned for hours, if at all, with doors that don't close properly, lights that don't work, and there aren't enough of them, with endless queues especially just before landing. So try to imagine the panic when not one, but all ten toilets on a flight were completely blocked and unusable. Unbelievable but true …

This happened recently on a Cathay Pacific flight from Riyadh to Hong Kong. All of the ten toilets on board the Airbus plane became blocked soon after take-off. Passengers wandered from one toilet to the other until the truth became obvious. There was chaos on board, with passengers demanding a rapid solution. The cabin crew's job of making passengers comfortable suddenly became impossible. When the captain made an announcement that he had decided to make an unscheduled landing at the nearest international airport, there was considerable relief on board. The flight landed in Mumbai.

> **'You would be amazed what we find in the pipes when we clean the system.'**

But Cathay's problems didn't end there. Within ten days, half the toilets on another two flights to Hong Kong became blocked. This time the problems were discovered before take-off; the flights went ahead, but the number of passengers had to be restricted.

Airline toilets use high-speed pipes to take waste at up to 110km/h into a holding tank, which is then emptied between flights. Airbus engineers are now fitting new toilet pipes to the airline's fleet, and carrying out deep cleaning. They believe they have solved the problem.

Cathay Pacific spokeswoman Carolyn Leung said that although the exact cause of the blockages was unclear, passengers themselves may be partly to blame. 'You would be amazed what we find in the pipes when we clean the system – not just paper towels, but medicine bottles, socks, items of clothing and even children's stuffed toys,' she said.

As for the Hong Kong flight diverted to Mumbai, the cabin crew had never been so delighted to hear the captain say, 'Cabin crew, cabin crew, seats for landing.'

Glossary

to block to stop something moving through
a fleet all the planes belonging to an airline
a blockage something which gets stuck; an obstruction
pipes tubes which carry liquid or waste
to be to blame to be at fault

UNIT 10 Saying goodbye

Arriving at the gate and disembarking the passengers

SPEAKING **1** **Work with a partner. Discuss the questions about what happens after the plane has landed.**

1 What do passengers usually want to do once the plane has landed?
2 What are some of the safety issues associated with disembarking passengers?
3 Why is it important to smile and say goodbye to passengers?
4 What special needs do passengers sometimes have?
5 What do cabin crew have to do themselves after the passengers have left the plane?

LISTENING **2** **The purser, Ted, is about to make the final announcement while the plane is taxiing to the gate in Boston. Before you listen, answer these questions.**

1 How do you expect the purser to begin his announcement?
2 What kind of information does the purser usually give?
3 What do the rest of the cabin crew do during the announcement?
4 What do you expect the purser to say about safety at this point?
5 How do you expect this last announcement to the passengers to end?

AUDIO 10.1 **Now listen and compare your answers.**

3 Listen to the final announcement again and fill in the missing words.

Ladies and gentlemen, on ¹_____ of the captain and the ²_____ crew we would like to welcome you to Boston, where the local time is 14.55.

For your safety, please remain seated with your seatbelt fastened, leaving all ³_____ of hand luggage safely ⁴_____ , until the seatbelt signs have been switched off. Before you leave the aircraft, please ⁵_____ that you have all your ⁶_____ items and hand-luggage with you. Please be careful when opening overhead lockers as items may fall out causing ⁷_____ .

We would like to remind you that smoking is not permitted until you've reached a ⁸_____ smoking area outside the terminal building. We would also like to ⁹_____ all passengers that mobile phones should not be switched on until the seatbelt signs have been turned off.

As the captain told you, it is very cold outside so I suggest you have your coats ¹⁰_____ for when you get outside the terminal!

We ¹¹_____ you a very pleasant stay or a safe journey if you are continuing your journey. We hope to see you again in the future. Goodbye.

PRONUNCIATION

AUDIO 10.2

4 Listen and repeat these phrases from the announcement.

➤ the entire crew   ➤ safely stowed   ➤ please be careful   ➤ terminal building
➤ the local time   ➤ please ensure   ➤ designated area

SPEAKING

5 Work with a partner. Take turns to practise making the final announcement. Use information about the places you fly to. Try to do it from memory or from notes.

LANGUAGE FOCUS

MAKING A RECOMMENDATION

Study these sentences.

I suggest (that) you have your coats ready for when you get outside the terminal!
I suggest (that) you take the airport bus into the city centre.
I suggest (that) you don't get up immediately but wait a few moments.

6 Work with a partner. What arrangements might need to be made before you can disembark disabled or elderly passengers, or passengers with special needs? What about unaccompanied children? Practise dealing with these types of passenger. Use the phrases below to help you.

➤ I suggest that you wait until all the passengers have disembarked.
➤ Would you mind staying in your seats until the wheelchairs arrive?
➤ Just stay in your seat for a little, and then someone will come and take you into the airport.
➤ It's better to wait until everyone has left the plane.

7 With your partner, decide which of these things it is important that you do before leaving the plane. Put a tick (✓).

a Check there are no passengers still in their seats.
b Check that the toilets are clean.
c Collect all customs paperwork from the galley.
d Make sure all personal items are in your carry-on bag.
e Check under the seats for forgotten passenger items.

8 Work in groups. Practise leaving the aircraft one by one and saying goodbye to the cabin crew. Rotate the roles so that everyone plays the flight attendant. Use the phrases below. Remember to be polite and friendly. You want the passengers to fly with you again!

➤ Thank you for flying with us, sir.   ➤ Enjoy your trip.
➤ Goodbye, madam.   ➤ Look forward to seeing you again soon.
➤ Have a good holiday.   ➤ Have a good day, Mr Gerighty.

Taking part in the crew debriefing

  Answer the questions about crew debriefings.

1 Where do debriefings usually take place?
  a on the plane
  b on the transit bus
  c in the terminal
2 What is the point of such meetings?
  a to relax together after the flight
  b to review the flight and any incidents
  c to finish writing reports and completing the paperwork
3 Who attends these meetings?
  a only senior crew members
  b the captain and the purser
  c all the flight crew and cabin crew
4 Why are they important?
  a They are necessary for crew resource management.
  b It's company policy to hold them.
  c They are part of an essential ongoing safety review.

 LISTENING AUDIO 10.3 **Listen to the captain's debriefing and answer the questions. You will hear the captain, the purser, Ted, and flight attendant, Leila, speaking.**

1 Why does the captain say the meeting will be short?
2 How does the captain know that the passengers' safety was well managed?
3 What two incidents does Ted want to discuss?
4 Why were Hemal and Jutta slow in securing the cabin and galley?
5 What does the 'Fasten seatbelts' sign mean for the cabin crew?
6 What should Leila have done?
7 During the turbulence, what happened to the trolley in the cabin?
8 What will Leila do next time? Are the sentences true (T) or false (F)?
  a She will improve communication with her team.
  b She will check that her team have heard the announcement.
  c She will tell the purser or captain when the cabin and galley are secure.
  d She will do the job herself to speed up the service shut-down.
  e She will make sure that the cabin and galley are secured as quickly as possible.

LANGUAGE FOCUS

SHOULD

Study these sentences.

We **should talk** about two incidents now.
You **should act** more promptly in future.
You **shouldn't continue** serving food next time.

Talking about the past
You **should've shut** down the service immediately.
You **should've told** them to stop.
I **should've communicated** better.
We **shouldn't have been** late.

PRONUNCIATION

 AUDIO 10.4

3 Listen and repeat the sentences in *Language focus*.

SPEAKING

4 Think back to previous incidents in your flying career. What kinds of things have gone wrong? Use *should / shouldn't* and *should have (done) / shouldn't have (done)* to talk about these incidents.

5 Work in pairs or small groups. Discuss what you think makes the cabin and flight crew into a successful team. Match these words and phrases with their meanings and use them in your discussions.

1	teamwork	**a**	looking after passengers
2	good communication	**b**	knowing precisely each other's roles
3	customer care	**c**	working for each other
4	problem-solving	**d**	taking action
5	crew coordination	**e**	talking to each other
6	decision-making	**f**	working out how best to do things

Case study

READING

1 **Read *Fear and heroism aboard Flight 253* opposite and answer the questions.**

1 What happened? When exactly during the flight did it happen?
2 Describe the explosive and how the man concealed it on board.
3 How did the passengers and crew react?

SPEAKING

2 **Work with a partner. Answer these questions and discuss the threat of terrorism and airport security.**

1 How do you think the man in the text managed to pass all the security checks? Has airport security changed since this incident? If so, in what ways?
2 What do you think about the crew's reaction to this incident? Have you been trained for such possibilities?

LISTENING

 AUDIO 10.5

3 **Listen to Shon Davis as she answers these questions. Make notes about what she says.**

1 'Has the threat of terrorism changed the flight attendant's job?'
2 'When the plane touches down, is that the end of your duties?'
3 'Is the flight attendant's job the same today as it was in the past?'

4 **Listen again and answer the questions.**

1 List the things that Shon says flight attendants are expected to check.
2 Which passengers does she say are the last to leave the aircraft?
3 List four of the adjectives she uses to describe the flight attendant's job.

SPEAKING

5 **Work with a partner. Discuss these questions.**

1 What happens once the flight has landed? When do the cabin crew leave the aircraft? What about the purser and the flight crew?
2 What makes you feel that you have done a good job after a flight?
3 Does the fear of terrorism make you want to be an even better professional, or does it make you think about changing your job?
4 Do you keep a diary or journal of your different flights, where you make a note of your experiences? Why? / Why not?
5 Being a flight attendant used to be a dream job. Do you think it still is? If not, what has changed?

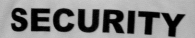

SECURITY

Fear and heroism aboard Flight 253

The flight was long and uneventful, at least until the final few minutes. First came a strange popping sound, followed by silence. Then came the unmistakable smell of smoke, and passengers began to shout and scream.

'People were just running, and they were scared,' said Veena Saigal, a passenger who saw the fire six rows behind her. 'They were running toward the centre of the plane, running to get away from the flames.'

Jasper Schuring, from Amsterdam, jumped over several other passengers to reach the fire in row 19. He burned his fingers as he grabbed a piece of very hot plastic held by Umar Farouk Abdulmutallab, the Nigerian man accused of trying to bring down the passenger jet with a home-made explosive device. Schuring held Abdulmutallab. Other passengers used blankets and a flight attendant rushed to the scene with a fire extinguisher to put out the flames.

Witnesses said that Abdulmutallab had spent about twenty minutes in the toilet before returning to seat 19A complaining of an upset stomach. He pulled a blanket over his head. Then came the loud and sudden popping sound.

'We heard a pop, then the smell and the reality kicked in for all of us. The reality was the fear in the flight attendants' eyes,' said businessman Charles Keepman.

Flight attendant Dionne Ransom-Monroe asked the man what was in his pocket, and he replied, 'Explosive device.' The explosive device on Abdulmutallab was a six-inch packet of high explosives called PETN, along with a syringe. It was hidden in Abdulmutallab's underpants.

When the fire was out, Schuring marched Abdulmutallab to the front of the plane, helped by a flight attendant. Abdulmutallab said nothing and did not resist. 'He looked like a normal guy,' Schuring said. 'It's just hard to believe he was actually trying to blow up this plane.'

The captain told passengers over the intercom: 'There was an incident, and everything is under control. It is over. Fasten your seatbelts. We are about to land.'

The incident had lasted just a few minutes, but the experience left many passengers upset long after the aircraft safely landed.

> 'We heard a pop, then the smell and the reality kicked in for all of us. The reality was the fear in the flight attendants' eyes.'

> 'They were running toward the centre of the plane, running to get away from the flames.'

Glossary

to pop to make a short, explosive sound
to bring down to cause to crash
to blow up to explode; to destroy in an explosion
an explosive device something designed to explode
to put out to extinguish; to stop from burning
a syringe a tube used for pushing out liquid
to march someone to make someone walk with you

81

 **UNIT 1**

The pre-flight briefing

Study the main units first, especially the *Listening* sections, so that you become very familiar with the content, vocabulary and language used. Then do these *Self Study* exercises. If there's anything you are unsure about, don't hesitate to go back to the main unit and have another look. Don't forget that the audio scripts from all the *Listening* exercises are in the back of the book to help you, too.

Meeting colleagues

1 Complete the conversation between two flight attendants. Use these words.

> met ■ how ■ pleased ■ about ■ hello
> meet ■ bad ■ know

Jared	¹_____ Soo-Min, ²_____ are you?
Soo-Min	Fine. What ³_____ you?
Jared	Not too ⁴_____. This is Ana, by the way. Do you ⁵_____ her?
Soo-Min	No, we haven't ⁶_____. ⁷_____ to meet you, Ana.
Ana	Nice to ⁸_____ you, Soo-Min.

 2 Complete the sentences. Use these job titles.

> flight attendants ■ purser ■ first officer
> galley leader ■ captain ■ cabin supervisor

1 The _____ is in command of the plane.
2 The _____ are there to ensure the safety and comfort of passengers.
3 There is a _____ in charge of each section of the aircraft.
4 All the cabin crew report to the _____.
5 With the captain in the cockpit is the _____.
6 The _____ is responsible for the meals service in their sector.

3 Match the situations with the expressions.

1 meeting a friend _____
2 meeting a colleague for the first time _____
3 telling someone your name _____
4 the purser greeting the cabin crew _____
5 greeting the captain _____
6 greeting a colleague you've worked with before _____

a Nice to meet you again.
b Hello, how are you all?
c Good morning, Captain.
d Hi, how's it going?
e My name's Paula.
f Pleased to meet you.

4 Reorder the letters to find items in the flight attendant's carry-on bag.

1 dricet dsarc _____
2 okob _____
3 sganizame _____
4 ekam-pu agb _____
5 saprostp _____
6 syke _____
7 htsotorbuh _____
8 libome hopne _____

Finding out about the flight

5 Fill in the missing words from the captain's briefing about expected stormy weather.

I just wanted to warn the crew of some moderate ¹t_____ during the flight – this is due to strong ²w_____ and ³s_____ over the Atlantic. We anticipate this bad ⁴w_____ about three and a half hours into the flight today.

6 Write questions to ask the meaning of the words and expressions 1–8. Then write answers with the correct replies a–h.

What does SEP mean? It means Standard Emergency Procedures.
What are … They're … / What's … It's …

1 cockpit procedures
2 strapped in
3 roster
4 shuttle
5 long-haul
6 log book
7 passport
8 stowage areas

a a long flight
b flight deck rules and routines
c a crew bus to the aircraft
d wearing seatbelts
e where we put things away
f personal identity document
g where we write things down
h a list of names and duties

1 _____
2 _____
3 _____
4 _____
5 _____
6 _____
7 _____
8 _____

LOG BOOK

Each of the ten Self Study sections in this book contains a log book page where you can record ...

➤ useful things you learn during the course
➤ interesting things that happen during lessons or when you are studying independently
➤ your thoughts about what you are learning and how you are improving your English
➤ things that are easy or difficult for you.

Use the questions to help you with ideas for your log book.

Think about a time you arrived late for a pre-flight briefing.

➤ What did you say?
➤ How did you find out about what you had missed?
➤ What do you remember about the flight which followed?

How do you prepare for a pre-flight briefing?

➤ Do you check the aircraft configuration and its safety features?
➤ Do you prepare for security questions?
➤ What kind of questions do you usually ask?

The pre-flight briefing is also a time for meeting colleagues.

➤ Is this important before the flight? Why?
➤ Do you look forward to meeting new colleagues?
➤ Do you also speak to the flight crew?

Notes

_____

_____

_____

_____

_____

_____

_____

_____

_____

_____

_____

In the space age, man will be able to go around the world in two hours — one hour for flying and one hour to get to the airport.

Neil H McElroy (US Secretary of Defense 1957–9)

Welcome on board

Welcoming passengers

1 Complete the conversations. Use these words.

> exit ■ course ■ front ■ welcome ■ check
> boarding ■ together ■ change ■ flight ■ seats

1 **A** Welcome on board. Your [1]_____ pass, please.
  B Here it is.
  A Thank you. You're in the [2]_____ row. It's half-way down the aisle, on the right.

2 **A** Hello, good morning. Can I [3]_____ your boarding passes?
  B Yes, of [4]_____. If possible we would like to sit [5]_____.
  A OK. Please take these [6]_____ for now and I'll try to [7]_____ them for you when all the passengers have boarded the plane. The [8]_____ isn't full today.
  B Thanks a lot.

3 **A** Hello, sir. [9]_____.
  B Thanks. Sorry I'm a little late.
  A No problem. You're in seat 3B. It's on the left at the [10]_____ of the aircraft.

2 Match the action words 1–6 with the phrases a–f.

1	greet	**a**	everyone to switch off mobile phones
2	check	**b**	the exit row is clear
3	make sure that	**c**	that all seatbelts are fastened
4	close	**d**	passengers
5	show	**e**	the overhead lockers
6	tell	**f**	the safety instruction card

3 Make these sentences into polite requests. Use the words in brackets to help you.

1 I want to see your boarding pass. (Could I ...)
  _____

2 Put your bag in the overhead locker. (Would you ...)
  _____

3 Switch off your phone now. (Could you ...)
  _____

4 What's your seat number? (Can I ...)
  _____

5 Sit there please. (Would ...)
  _____

6 Fold your tray table. (... mind ...)
  _____

Settling passengers in their seats

4 Read the conversation between a flight attendant and passengers boarding a flight. Then answer the questions below using phrases from the conversation.

Passenger 1 Excuse me, there are four of us in the same family. My son and daughter are with me here, but my husband is in a seat three rows behind us. We need four seats together. Is it possible to change seats with someone near us?

Flight attendant Yes, I understand. Everyone is boarding just now, but I'll check this out for you. Let me see what I can do. I'll try my best.

Passenger 1 Thanks, I appreciate that. Please try.

Flight attendant Of course. I'll come back as soon as I can.

Flight attendant (to another passenger) Excuse me, sir, are you alone?

Passenger 2 No, we're together. This is my wife.

Flight attendant Oh, yes, of course. Sorry to bother you. (to another passenger) Excuse me, madam, is this your seat?

Passenger 3 Yes, why?

Flight attendant Would you mind changing it with the father of these children? The family want to be together.

Passenger 3 Well ... er ... that depends. Where is his seat?

Flight attendant It's just three rows back and it's also an aisle seat.

Passenger 3 Oh, that's good, then – no problem. I want an aisle seat, too.

Flight attendant Great. Many thanks. It makes all the difference.

Passenger 3 My pleasure.

Flight attendant (to family) There you are. That was easy.

1 What does the mother ask?
  _____

2 Why can't the flight attendant change the seat immediately?
  _____

3 What does the family need?
  _____

4 Where does the mother say her husband's seat is?
  _____

5 What reason does the woman give for agreeing to change seats?
  _____

5 Complete the flight attendant's description of how things work. Use these words.

> button ■ menu ■ press ■ down ■ reading
> select ■ how ■ then ■ volume

This is ¹_____ the TV handset works. First, press the ²_____ button and this gives you a choice of options. You can choose from these options by going up or ³_____, like this. So, let's ⁴_____ 'Films'. ⁵_____ you get another choice, so it's 'Select' again. This one. OK? Oh, and you have the ⁶_____ control on the left here. And this is for your ⁷_____ light. Just ⁸_____ on and off. And if you need anything, don't forget the call ⁹_____. This one. All right?

Demonstrating safety procedures and checking before take-off

6 How well do you know the safety instructions? Fill in the missing words from this extract. Listen to audio 2.7 to check your answers.

Listen ¹_____ to the following safety instructions.

You will find a safety ²_____ card in the pocket in front of you. Please read this carefully before take-off and ³_____ yourself with the emergency exits and procedures on ⁴_____ this Boeing 777S.

When the seatbelt ⁵_____ is on, you must fasten your seatbelt. To do this, insert the metal fitting into the ⁶_____ – like this, and tighten by ⁷_____ the strap – like this. To undo the seatbelt, ⁸_____ the buckle – like this. We suggest you keep the seatbelt fastened ⁹_____ the flight.

There are several emergency exits on this aircraft. They are being ¹⁰_____ out to you now. Please take a few moments now to locate your ¹¹_____ exit. It may be behind you. If you are sitting in an emergency exit, you must know how to ¹²_____ the door in an emergency and when instructed to do so by the crew.

7 Put the words in the correct order to make requests. Then match the requests with illustrations a–h on page 17.

1 seatbelt please your sir fasten.

_____

2 upright the your in please seat position put.

_____

3 seatbelt just I your can check?

_____

4 mind you off would computer switching your?

_____

5 phone off please switch your.

_____

6 table sir up your you could put?

_____

7 bag mind the putting in overhead would your locker you?

_____

8 this read please notice.

_____

LOG BOOK

Do you enjoy welcoming passengers on board your flight?

➤ How do you show this?
➤ Are you nervous of certain types of passenger?
➤ Do you recognize regular types of passenger?

What do you say to welcome different passengers? What do you say to ...

➤ children?   ➤ older people?   ➤ business travellers?

Have you become an expert in the safety instructions before take-off?

➤ Do you practise making the announcement?
➤ Do you try to improve your demonstration of the safety instructions?
➤ Do you say anything to passengers who don't listen to the instructions?

Notes

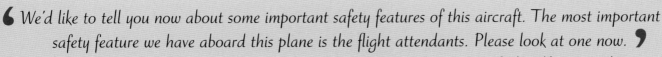

We'd like to tell you now about some important safety features of this aircraft. The most important safety feature we have aboard this plane is the flight attendants. Please look at one now.

After take-off and into the flight

Making the first announcements

 1 **Read the announcement about beginning the refreshment service. Find words and phrases which have the same meaning as 1–8 below. Then practise saying the announcement.**

'Ladies and gentlemen, we shall shortly be coming through the cabin with hot and cold drinks and light refreshments. Kindly look at the menu card in the seat pocket in front of you and have your orders ready. The exact change would be appreciated. This is a short flight and we'd like to serve everyone on board, so please remain seated if possible during the service. Thank you, and enjoy the flight.'

1 in a few moments _____
2 down the aisles _____
3 snacks _____
4 Please be good enough to _____
5 a list of items to eat and drink _____
6 correct amount of money _____
7 less than 1.5 hours of flying time _a_____
8 stay in your seats _____

2 **There are eight mistakes in the following announcement. Can you find and correct them all?**

'Ladies and men, it's great have you on board. The seatbelt sign has been switched. You can to move around the cabin now. In a few moments we shall be come through cabin with refreshments. Please be ready your order. We'd really appreciate if you had the exact change for your purchases.'

Getting started

 3 **Fatima, the senior flight attendant on board, is talking to her colleague. Fill in the gaps using these words.**

> short ■ seated ■ trolleys ■ minutes
> aisles ■ time ■ sign ■ service

'OK, the seatbelt ¹_____ is off. This is a
²_____ flight, only an hour and 25 minutes. Fifteen minutes have already passed, and we have to finish the
³_____ about 20 ⁴_____ before landing.
We've got 169 passengers and there are just four of us. So, no ⁵_____ to waste.

'Oh dear, I asked people to remain ⁶_____ and look, there are passengers moving in the ⁷_____ already. Oh well! Let's get the ⁸_____ out and do our best.'

 4 **Answer the questions about what Fatima said in exercise 3.**

1 At what stage of the flight is this happening?
_____

2 How much time is there for the service?
_____

3 What did Fatima ask the passengers to do during the service?
_____

4 What are some of the passengers doing?
_____

5 What do the flight attendants have to do first of all?
_____

Helping to settle passengers

5 **Read these four exchanges on a long-haul flight. Choose the best phrase from the list to finish each one.**

> Let me get them a snack.
> Of course, no problem at all. I'll be right back.
> Just give me a few minutes to get that ready for you.
> I'll be back with a new pair in a few minutes.

1 **Flight attendant** Is everything all right, madam?
Passenger Yes, fine, thanks. Can I have a glass of water?
Flight attendant _____

2 **Flight attendant** What can I do for you?
Passenger My earphones don't work.
Flight attendant Oh dear, let me change them. _____

3 **Flight attendant** Did you call, madam?
Passenger Yes, sorry to bother you, but my children are a little hungry.
Flight attendant No bother at all. _____

4 **Flight attendant** How are you now?
Passenger I'm still a bit nervous, but I'd love a cup of tea.
Flight attendant With pleasure. _____

6 Complete these expressions used when settling passengers.

1 _____ worry, you'll be fine.
2 _____ me help you with that.
3 Is everything _____ _____?
4 Are you _____ better now?
5 Push the _____ button if you need anything.
6 Of _____, no problem at all.
7 Can I get you anything _____?
8 I'll be _____ in five minutes.
9 I do _____, madam. I'll get your blanket now.
10 No _____, sir. I'll do that now.
11 Yes, that's fine. Go _____.
12 Can I _____ you, madam?

7 Which of these phrases could you use when talking to a passenger who is difficult to understand?

1 Say again, please.
2 Excuse me, I didn't catch that.
3 You are impossible to understand.
4 I don't know what you're saying.
5 Sorry, please say that again.
6 Could you repeat that, please?

LOG BOOK

Think about a time you helped to settle a passenger on a long-haul flight.

➤ What did you do to help them?
➤ What language did you use?
➤ Have you learned any new expressions that you could use in the future?

Think about a bad experience during or immediately after take-off.

➤ What happened?
➤ How did you and your colleagues react?
➤ What would you do differently the next time you had a similar experience?

Think about when there was a problem with the refreshment service on a short-haul flight.

➤ What happened?
➤ What did you say and do to resolve the problem?

Notes

_____
_____
_____
_____
_____
_____
_____
_____
_____

❝ We have now reached our cruising altitude, so I am going to switch the seatbelt sign off.
Feel free to move about as you wish, but please stay inside the plane until we land —
it's a bit cold outside and if you walk on the wings, it affects the flight pattern. ❞ A pilot

Food and drinks

Giving a choice

 1 Complete the conversation between a flight attendant and a passenger during the meals service. Use these words.

> special ■ menu ■ tray ■ starter ■ ask ■ full
> choose ■ pre-order ■ much ■ course

Passenger Excuse me, can I ¹_____ a question about the ²_____, please?

Flight attendant By all means.

Passenger It's not for me, it's for my daughter. This is a ³_____ meal, isn't it?

Flight attendant Yes, that's right – look, it says '⁴_____, main ⁵_____ and dessert'.

Passenger I thought so, but that's too ⁶_____ for my daughter. Do you have a children's menu?

Flight attendant Yes, we do, but you have to ⁷_____ ⁸_____ meals.

Passenger What a pity.

Flight attendant Look, it's not a problem, I'll bring her the full ⁹_____ and she can pick and ¹⁰_____ what she likes. She will probably give you the vegetables!

Passenger You're right. That's fine then. Thanks so much.

2 A full meal is a starter, main course and dessert. Put these items from the menu in the correct column. Which one does not go in any of the three columns?

> egg mayonnaise ■ chocolate pudding
> smoked salmon ■ chicken tikka ■ tuna salad
> fish in white sauce ■ lemon sponge
> tomatoes and olives ■ beef bourguignon
> fruit salad ■ lasagne ■ salade niçoise ■ apple pie
> chicken satay and rice ■ grapes ■ seafood salad
> lamb and couscous ■ cheese and biscuits ■ ice cream

Starter	Main course	Dessert

Serving drinks

3 Study the list of drinks. At what stage of the meals service would you normally offer them? Write *B* (before), *D* (during), or *A* (after) the meal.

1	Perrier	_____	8	beer	_____
2	apple juice	_____	9	mango juice	_____
3	Sauvignon Blanc	_____	10	cappuccino	_____
4	peppermint tea	_____	11	diet Coke	_____
5	port	_____	12	still water	_____
6	tomato juice	_____	13	champagne	_____
7	Earl Grey tea	_____	14	cognac	_____

4 Put the words in the correct order to make questions that flight attendants and passengers ask.

1 drink, you madam to what like would ?

_____

2 sir you to like would drink, something ?

_____

3 for drink, you would care sir a ?

_____

4 I can sir you, what get ?

_____

5 I water of have glass a could ?

_____

6 please cold I beer, have a can ?

_____

Duty-free sales

5 Match the questions and answers about duty-free sales.

1 Any duty-free items? Duty free? _____
2 Have you got any toys for children? _____
3 How much do these scarves cost? _____
4 Have you got any aftershave? _____
5 How much is this brooch? _____
6 How do you want to pay? _____
7 Sure. Anything else? _____
8 Excuse me, did you give me a receipt? _____

a Fifty-four dollars. They're made of silk.
b We have a special promotion on jewellery: it's only $39 instead of $49.
c My mistake, I do apologize.
d Yes, I'd like to see ladies' perfumes, please.
e In cash in local currency, please.
f Yes, we've got two: a model aircraft and a teddy bear.
g Yes, we have a range of gifts for men.
h That's all, thank you.

6 Complete the crossword with items from the duty-free trolley.

Across

2 You use a travel _____ for shaving.
4 Scotland's most famous alcoholic drink.
5 A ladies' gift that smells nice.
8 These are made from cocoa beans.
9 A strong alcoholic drink from Russia.
10 A _____ bear is a favourite soft toy for children.

Down

1 You can smoke these.
3 A pleasant-smelling gift for a man.
6 Make-up for the eyes.
7 Rings, necklaces, bracelets, etc.

LOG BOOK

The in-flight meals service is the best moment to get to know the passengers.

➤ What do you think? Is this true, or is it just about serving meals and nothing else?
➤ Do you have time to talk to passengers about their travel, holidays, and so on?
➤ Do you think most passengers appreciate the meals service?

What about difficult passengers who complain?

➤ What do you say if there is no choice of meal left?
➤ What do you say to a passenger who pre-ordered a meal, but it hasn't been recorded?
➤ What do you say to someone who says, 'It's awful, I can't eat this, and it's cold'?

What is your experience of selling duty-free goods?

➤ Do you enjoy being a sales person?
➤ What do passengers buy? What is your most interesting experience?
➤ What do you say if you haven't got the goods someone asks for?

Notes

_____
_____
_____
_____
_____
_____
_____
_____
_____
_____
_____

❝ *An aeroplane is a great place to diet.* ❞
Anonymous

Identifying passenger problems

 A passenger has pressed the call button. Read the conversation and answer the questions below.

Flight attendant Hello. Can I help you, madam?

Passenger The cabin is really cold. One of your colleagues said he was going to check the cabin temperature. That was 15 minutes ago and it's still freezing. I hope it's not going to be like this for the whole flight.

Flight attendant I'm really sorry, madam. You're right; it isn't very warm at the moment! I'm afraid it often takes about 20 minutes for the cabin to acclimatize after take-off, but it shouldn't be long now before it begins to feel warmer. Meanwhile, can I get you a blanket and maybe a hot beverage?

Passenger Good – I'm really cold! I don't need a drink, but I would like another blanket, please, and one for my husband, too.

Flight attendant OK. I'll be back in just a moment, madam. *(comes back)* I've just checked the cabin temperature and it is set at 23°C, which is normal. I've switched it up to 25°C to help speed things up and I'll pop back to see you in about five minutes to check you are a bit more comfortable. Would that be all right?

Passenger Thanks very much. Oh, and could I have a hot chocolate after all?

Flight attendant Of course. I'll get that for you now.

1 What's the problem?

2 What should the temperature in the cabin be?

3 What's the solution?

4 How long does it usually take for the cabin to get warm?

5 Find another word in the conversation that means 'drink'.

6 Would the woman prefer a hot drink or a blanket?

7 What does the flight attendant promise to do?

8 What does the woman change her mind about and ask for?

 Find phrases in the conversation in exercise 1 which mean the same as 1–5 below.

1 What can I do for you?

2 I do apologize.

3 Would you like ...?

4 I'll come back soon.

5 Is that OK?

Dealing with problems

 Listen to the four problems on audio 5.4. Are the sentences true (T) or false (F)?

1 There is a traveller who has transit problems.
2 A passenger is cold.
3 Another passenger is hungry.
4 There is a sick mother with her daughter.
5 Passenger 1 is worried about her baggage.
6 Passenger 2 has a sandwich.
7 Passenger 3 must wait 20 minutes for a blanket.
8 Passenger 4's daughter has a high temperature and a bad headache.
9 The flight attendants solve all four problems.

Flight attendants cannot deal with every problem straight away, so they use *will* or *I'll* and offer to do something as soon as they can. Listen to audio 5.4 again and write what the flight attendant says when offering help with the four problems.

1 the transit problem

2 the hungry passenger

3 the cold passenger

4 the sick daughter

Saying sorry

 5 **Match the passengers' comments and requests with the replies.**

1 I'd like the beef, please.
2 Have you got any paracetamol?
3 I'd like some tea, please.
4 I rang the call button several times.
5 The sound of the film still doesn't work.
6 This meal's cold.
7 I'd like the fish, please.

a Certainly. Earl Grey or English Breakfast?
b I do apologize, we've been so busy.
c I am sorry, but we've run out of beef.
d I'm really sorry, we've only got beef left.
e I can only apologize. I'll change it.
f Sorry about that. Try pushing this button.
g Yes, but I'm afraid I can't give it to you without a doctor.

LOG BOOK

Think about the usual in-flight passenger problems.

➤ What are these minor problems?
➤ What language do you use to solve them?
➤ Are you tired of giving the same replies, or is every case different?

Think about one particular problem you had to deal with.

➤ What happened?
➤ In what way was this problem different from others?
➤ Were you satisfied that you dealt with it in the best possible way?

Think about in-flight problems in general.

➤ Does your airline train you to manage problems and difficult passengers?
➤ Do problems spoil the flight experience for both the flight attendants and the passengers?
➤ Is dealing with passenger problems the worst side of your job, or simply what you are trained to expect?

Notes

❛ *There are only two emotions in a plane: boredom and terror.* ❜
Orson Welles

Is there a doctor on board?

Dealing with an on-board accident

1 Listen to audio 6.1 and 6.2 and then complete the missing words in this summary of the incident.

The incident happened during ¹t_____ after the captain asked everyone to ²r_____ to their seats. Leila rushed to the lady and saw she was ³h_____ and her ⁴h_____ was bleeding. Another passenger said a ⁵l_____ had fallen out of the overhead ⁶l_____ and hit her on the head. She was ⁷u_____. Leila asked her ⁸c_____, Hemal, to get the first aid ⁹k_____ quickly and then spoke to the lady, who ¹⁰o_____ her eyes.

She said she felt ¹¹d_____ , but she was not in ¹²p_____. Leila gave her a ¹³g_____ of water and told her the ¹⁴c_____ was not serious. She cleaned up the ¹⁵w_____ and put a ¹⁶d_____ over it and asked her to hold a ¹⁷c_____ against her forehead. The lady said she was feeling ¹⁸f_____ and Leila helped her to her ¹⁹s_____ and ²⁰f_____ her seatbelt.

2 Which items in the list would you find in the first aid kit for cabin crew (not the full medical kit used by doctors and nurses or qualified senior crew)?

➤ stethoscope
➤ needles
➤ diarrhoea tablets
➤ cardiopulmonary resuscitation (CPR) masks
➤ automatic external defibrillator (AED)
➤ bandages
➤ compresses
➤ scissors
➤ face masks
➤ approved medication
➤ syringes
➤ latex gloves
➤ painkillers
➤ triangular bandages
➤ antiseptic wipes
➤ wound dressings
➤ oxygen
➤ safety pins

Dealing with a serious medical incident

3 In a serious medical incident such as a heart attack, which of actions a–l below would you take? Which would you definitely not take?

a Get the passenger a glass of water.
b Ask any travelling companions about the passenger's medication, medical history, etc.
c Tell a colleague to inform the captain.
d Ask if there is a doctor on board.
e Tell a colleague to get the oxygen, mask and defibrillator ready.
f Tell other passengers to make room.
g Carry the passenger into Business class.
h Lie the passenger down and undo their clothing.
i Take the passenger's pulse.
j Prepare to administer CPR.
k Wait for the doctor.
l Leave the passenger and go and get another colleague.

4 Do you remember the standard response to medical problems? Write sentences 1–14 in the correct column.

CHECK (find out what is wrong)   *What's wrong?*
↓
CALL (describe, inform, get help)   *It's a heart attack. Tell the captain.*
↓
CARE (take action, take care)   *Give him some oxygen.*

1 How are you feeling?
2 Are you in pain?
3 He looks very sick.
4 Lie him down.
5 He's not breathing normally.
6 Make room, please.
7 Get the oxygen and defibrillator.
8 Where's the pain?
9 He's complaining of a pain in his chest.
10 Loosen his clothing.
11 Are you on any medication?
12 He says he's got chest pains.
13 Check his pulse.
14 Have you been sick before?

CHECK	
CALL	
CARE	

Reporting a medical incident

5 Complete the conversation describing the incident with the passenger who had a heart attack. Use the past simple form of these verbs.

arrive ▪ collapse ▪ loosen ▪ check ▪ report ▪ remain
decide ▪ ask ▪ administer ▪ suffer ▪ recommend

A What happened?

B A passenger ¹_____ and ²_____ a heart attack.

A What did the flight attendant do?

B She ³_____ him and ⁴_____ his clothing.

A What did she tell her colleague to get?

B She ⁵_____ for oxygen and a defibrillator.

A Did she tell the captain?

B Yes, she ⁶_____ the passenger's condition to the captain.

A And then?

B She ⁷_____ CPR and ⁸_____ with the passenger.

A Was there a doctor on board?

B Yes, he ⁹_____ quickly and ¹⁰_____ immediate hospitalization.

A What did the captain do?

B He ¹¹_____ to make an emergency landing.

LOG BOOK

What experience do you have of on-board medical incidents?

➤ What did you do to help the passenger(s)?

➤ What language did you use to find out the problem?

➤ Are there other expressions you could use in similar situations in the future?

Think about a serious incident you witnessed or assisted at.

➤ What happened?

➤ How did you and your colleagues react?

➤ What would you do differently the next time you had a similar experience?

Do you think you have sufficient training to deal with on-board medical incidents?

➤ Do you depend on your colleagues?

➤ Do you spend personal time improving your knowledge and first aid skills?

➤ Do you know how to ask the right questions? Can you use the right expressions to obtain information and describe sick passengers?

Notes

_____

_____

_____

_____

_____

_____

_____

_____

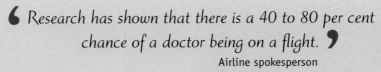

❛ *Research has shown that there is a 40 to 80 per cent chance of a doctor being on a flight.* ❜

Airline spokesperson

In-flight emergencies

Taking charge in an emergency

1   **Do you remember the pre-flight safety announcement? Fill in the key words and expressions. Listen to audio 2.7 and check your answers.**

There are several ¹_____ exits on this aircraft. They are being pointed out to you now. Please take a few moments now to ²_____ your nearest exit. It may be ³_____ you. If you are sitting in an emergency ⁴_____, you must know how to open the ⁵_____ in an emergency and when ⁶_____ to do so by the crew.

If we need to evacuate the aircraft, ⁷_____-level lighting will ⁸_____ you to the exits.

In the event of an emergency ⁹_____, you will hear 'Brace, brace' and you must ¹⁰_____ this position. Look at the card for the brace position.

Your life ¹¹_____ is under your seat. This is how you put it on.

If the ¹²_____ drops, an ¹³_____ mask will automatically drop from the ¹⁴_____ above your head. To start the ¹⁵_____ of oxygen, pull the mask towards you, put it firmly over your ¹⁶_____ and nose and secure the elastic ¹⁷_____ behind your head and ¹⁸_____ normally. If you are travelling with a child or a person who needs ¹⁹_____, put your mask on ²⁰_____ and then assist the other person.

2   **Match verbs 1–9 with phrases a–i to complete the instructions used in emergencies.**

1	Pull down	**a**	the brace position.
2	Place it	**b**	this red cord.
3	Stay in	**c**	the exit door.
4	Secure	**d**	your seats.
5	Locate	**e**	the oxygen mask.
6	Open	**f**	normally.
7	Adopt	**g**	the elastic band behind your head.
8	Pull on	**h**	your nearest exit.
9	Breathe	**i**	over your mouth and nose.

Preparing for an emergency evacuation

3 **The captain has decided to make an emergency landing in 20 minutes' time. He has just made an announcement to passengers. Are the sentences true (T) or false (F)?**

Passengers ...
1 can go to the toilets for the last time
2 must return to their seats immediately
3 must put all their bags in the lockers
4 must take their shoes off
5 must take up the brace position
6 must wait for instructions.

Cabin crew ...
7 will quickly collect any debris
8 will check that all seatbelts are fastened
9 will answer questions about the evacuation
10 will distribute disembarkation cards
11 will check the toilets
12 will sit down, strap in and wait for instructions.

4 **Listen to audio 7.4. Towards the end of the track, the purser gives instructions for what to do after landing. Number the instructions in the order you hear them.**

a _____ I repeat, leave all your personal hand-baggage behind.

b _____ Do not leave your seats until instructed to do so by your crew.

c _____ Ladies, remove high-heeled shoes as they may tear the slide.

d _____ Please remain seated and follow instructions given to you by your crew.

e _____ Leave all personal belongings behind.

f _____ When the seatbelt signs are switched off, make your way to your nearest exit.

Reporting an evacuation

5 **Report these instructions given by the purser.**

1 'Remain seated.'
The purser told the passengers to remain seated.

2 'Follow the instructions given to you by your crew.'
He told them ...

3 'Do not leave your seats until instructed.'

4 'Make your way to the nearest exit.'

5 'Ladies, take off your high-heeled shoes.'

6 'Leave all personal belongings behind.'

6 **Use the prompts to write a paragraph reporting what a passenger said about an emergency evacuation. Combine sentences using *and*, *but* and some of the linking words you learned in Unit 6.**

all the lights / go off / oxygen masks / come down

be / a lot of smoke in the cabin / everyone / be / in a panic

cabin crew / be / very calm / tell / everyone / sit down

they / shout / 'Go!' / we all / rush / to the slides

I / not have time / think about it / or even / take off / high-heeled shoes

everyone / be / safe, / some people / be / injured at the bottom of the slide

---

LOG BOOK

Think about your training for emergencies.

➤ Is saving lives in emergencies the most important part of all your training?
➤ Do you think you need more training, or are you ready for any emergency?
➤ Do you learn from reported incidents and discuss them with your colleagues?

Think about a real or simulated emergency you were involved in.

➤ What happened?
➤ How did you and your colleagues react?
➤ What would you do differently the next time you had a similar experience?

What do you think about the safety instructions, especially for an evacuation?

➤ Do passengers really know what to do? Or do they just panic?
➤ How do you prepare and train for such panic situations?
➤ Describe what happened in such an incident which you or your colleagues experienced. What did you say, or shout, to the passengers?

Notes

❝ *In the event of a sudden loss of cabin pressure, masks will descend from the ceiling. Stop screaming, grab the mask and pull it over your face. If you have a small child travelling with you, secure your mask before assisting with theirs. If you are travelling with more than one small child, pick your favourite.* ❞

Complaints and disruptive passengers

Responding to passenger complaints

1 Choose the best reply to these complaints.

1 I can't sit in the middle. I feel trapped and I need to exercise during a 14-hour flight.
   a Sorry, I do understand, but do get up and move around when you wish.
   b There are lots of others who are just like you, sorry.
   c Let me see if I can move you to another seat. Wait a moment, please.

2 I want to sit with my wife and children. When I checked in they promised me I could.
   a Check-in was wrong to promise you that.
   b I'll look into it and get back to you.
   c Can you sort it out yourself, please?

3 Only fish left? No thanks, I'm allergic to fish. We're the last to be served and now you tell me there's only fish. It's unacceptable.
   a I know, it happens often. I'm sorry.
   b Let me see what I can get you from Business class. I'll be back.
   c I'm really sorry, but what can I do?

4 Excuse me, this is almost cold. I can't eat it like this.
   a Sorry about that, let me heat it up for you. Just two minutes.
   b Really? No-one else has complained.
   c I'm sorry, I haven't got time to reheat it.

Dealing with complaints about other passengers

2 Match the sentence halves.

1 If you're still feeling sick,   _____
2 If there is still a problem,   _____
3 I'll find you another seat   _____
4 If the volume on the handset doesn't work,   _____
5 If you don't like the meal,   _____
6 I'll get the children some colouring books   _____

a I'll come back.
b I'll change it.
c if they'd like that.
d I'll get another one for you.
e if there is one.
f I'll get my colleague, who's a nurse.

3 Read the conversation between Josef and Hans. Can you fill in the missing words? Listen to audio 8.6 to check your answers.

Josef Hans, I [1]n_____ your help.
Hans What's the problem, Josef?
Josef Can you see that guy [2]s_____ in the middle with his arms [3]f_____?
Hans Yes. He looks [4]u_____ and angry.
Josef He is. He wants me to tell the group [5]b_____ him to keep quiet or else he is demanding a seat [6]c_____. I wondered if there were any seats vacant in the next cabin in case I have to re-seat him?
Hans Out of the question. The plane's full. There aren't any [7]s_____ seats anywhere.
Josef OK. I'll go over and [8]t_____ the group to quieten down.
Hans I think that's the best thing.
Josef I just hope they'll be reasonable!
Hans You'll be fine! Just use your usual charm and ask them to be a [9]l_____ quieter!
Josef Hans, if you see me struggling, please could you come over to help me?
Hans You'll be [10]f_____, don't worry. I'll keep an eye on you. If there is still a problem, then I'll come over.

4 Listen to audio 8.7 and answer the questions.

1 What does Josef have to do?
2 What 'special' thing does he ask for?
3 Are the people angry about the request?
4 What two reasons does Josef give them for being quiet?
5 What do they want in return for being quiet?

Managing disruptive passengers

5 A flight attendant is dealing with a disruptive passenger. Find and correct six errors.

Flight attendant *(to the disruptive passenger)* Sir, you have to stop shouting and you must to sit down, please. *(to another passenger)* Madam, I can see how upset are you. Would you coming to the back of the plane with, please? I am apologize, and please don't worry. Everything is in control and incidents like this are extremely rare.

6 **Read this short report. Then study the grid on the right and find seven key words from the report that are associated with disruptive passengers. Words can be →, ↓ or ↘.**

A	B	U	S	I	V	E	D	M	E
C	G	R	F	S	H	A	I	Q	U
F	I	G	H	T	L	U	S	B	C
Z	C	E	R	I	E	R	R	O	W
U	L	M	B	E	F	O	U	Y	T
N	U	N	F	K	S	A	P	D	U
R	G	Y	K	R	B	S	T	P	E
U	P	S	H	O	U	T	I	N	G
L	X	H	A	Z	C	A	V	V	O
Y	N	W	I	J	L	A	E	D	E

DISRUPTIVE PASSENGERS FORCE FLIGHT TO DIVERT

A fight between rival football fans forced a plane to make an emergency landing last Friday.

The men, aged 24 and 36, could not be restrained by cabin crew after they started fighting and shouting. They were abusive and rude to the flight attendants and aggressive and insulting to other passengers.

The captain decided to land quickly and the unruly pair were handed over to the police on arrival.

LOG BOOK

Think about passengers complaining.

➤ Is this the most challenging part of your job, or simply something you accept?

➤ Can you anticipate most complaints? What kind of complaints do you expect?

➤ Do you know what to say and, above all, how to say it to complaining passengers?

Think about passengers complaining about other passengers.

➤ How do you handle these situations? Think of several examples.

➤ What do you say? What is your usual expression to solve the problem?

➤ Are you a good referee? What are the qualities you need for these situations?

Think about passengers behaving badly.

➤ Have you or your colleagues had a recent experience of unruly passengers? What happened? What did you say?

➤ What would you do differently the next time you had a similar experience?

➤ Are you a good police officer, or do you prefer to be a diplomat?

Notes

❝ *Please be sure to take all of your belongings. If you're going to leave anything, please make sure it's something we'd like to have.* ❞

Cabin crew member

Preparing for landing

Making final announcements and checks

 1 Look at the list 1–14 of final checks. How many minutes before landing would you do these things? Write the numbers in the correct column below.

1 Check seatbelts are fastened.
2 Make sure bags are in overhead lockers.
3 Get strapped in for landing.
4 Complete paperwork.
5 Check again that electrical devices are switched off.
6 Collect headsets.
7 Make final checks.
8 Secure trolleys in the galleys.
9 Check tables are folded away, seat backs are upright, arm-rests are down.
10 Check no-one is in the toilets.
11 Clear bags from exit rows.
12 Clear up debris.
13 Signal 'cabin secure'.
14 Ask people to switch off electrical devices.

20 minutes before landing	10 minutes before landing	2 minutes before landing

 2 Rewrite the instruction using a pronoun instead of the noun.

1 Turn off your computer, please.
Turn it off, please.

2 Fold away your table now, please.

3 Put your bags in the overhead lockers.

4 Switch off your DVD player now, please.

5 Put your seat back upright, please.

6 Put your arm-rest down, please.

Giving information about delayed landings

 3 Choose the correct option in these phrases and sentences.

1 twenty minutes *for / to* landing
2 16.00 = *4 of the clock / 4 o'clock*
3 It *takes / is taking* three hours to get to Tenerife.
4 The flight *is lasting / lasts* seven and a half hours.
5 11.45 = *eleven forty-five / fifteen to twelve*
6 12.00 p.m. = *noon / midnight*
7 13.35 = *thirty-five past one / twenty-five to two*
8 Your *connecting / connected* flight is at 10.15.

 4 Complete the conversation. Use these words.

> when ■ the time ■ time ■ how much ■ how ■ about

Passenger 1 Excuse me, what's ¹_____ difference between Paris and Dubai?
Flight attendant Dubai is three hours ahead.
Passenger 1 So what ²_____ is it on the ground in Dubai now?
Flight attendant Let me see ... half past five.
Passenger 1 And, sorry to bother you again, ³_____ longer before we arrive?
Flight attendant Oh, a couple of hours or so yet.
Passenger 2 ⁴_____ exactly do we get there?
Flight attendant About half past seven in the evening, local time.
Passenger 2 Do you know ⁵_____ long it takes from the terminal to the city centre?
Flight attendant Yes, it takes ⁶_____ 40 minutes.

5 Fill in the gaps in this announcement by the first officer. Listen to audio 9.5 to check your answers.

Ladies and gentlemen, this is the first officer ¹_____. Unfortunately I have some ²_____ news for you. Air ³_____ Control has advised us that, ⁴_____ to a problem on the ground, we will be ⁵_____ for approximately 30 minutes or so. My ⁶_____ for any ⁷_____, but we'll get you on the ground as ⁸_____ as possible. In the ⁹_____, please keep your seatbelts ¹⁰_____.

Getting through the final ten minutes

6 Complete these questions about the final checks before landing.

1 _____ you d_____ the clearing in?
2 _____ she s_____ the trolley in the galley?
3 _____ he c_____ that the tables are upright?
4 _____ they c_____ all the headsets?
5 _____ you f_____ the bar paperwork?
6 _____ we c_____ the final checks?

7 Reorder the letters of the words in the box. Then use the words to complete the announcement below.

inmtue ■ prdspaet ■ nacbi ecwr ■ wosted
glhtfi cekd ■ kheccs ■ ucerse

'Cabin crew, ten minutes to landing, ten minutes to landing.'

The 'ten minutes to landing' is a call from the [1]_____ _____ to the [2]_____ _____. They will then make final [3]_____ and make sure that the cabin is [4]_____. All passengers must be seated with seatbelts fastened, and all bags must be [5]_____ away. The cabin crew can still move about for last-[6]_____ checks. Just before landing, they receive the 'Cabin crew, seats for landing' call. At that point, they must return to their seats and get [7]_____ in for landing.

LOG BOOK

Think about the last 20 minutes before landing.

➤ Is this the most stressful moment of the flight? Why?
➤ Is this when you see the best and the worst of your colleagues?
➤ Do you show by example, or tell others what to do?

Think about a bad experience you've had during the preparation for landing.

➤ What happened? How did you evaluate your own performance?
➤ What do you say to colleagues who perform badly? Do you get angry, or discuss things calmly?
➤ What do you say to passengers who are difficult at this time?

Think about the organization of these final 20 minutes.

➤ Is your routine always automatic? Do things work perfectly, as in your training?
➤ Who does what among the cabin crew and the flight crew?
➤ What do you think about when you hear 'Cabin crew, seats for landing'?

Notes
_____
_____
_____
_____
_____
_____
_____
_____

❛ *Weather at our destination is 60 degrees with some broken clouds, but we will try to have them fixed for you before we arrive.* ❜

A pilot

Arriving at the gate and disembarking the passengers

1 ▶ **Reorder the words to make sentences. Which one would you *not* normally say to passengers?**

1 wonderful a have holiday

_____

2 madam your trip enjoy

_____

3 home safe journey

_____

4 soon to you seeing look again forward

_____

5 was bad it such a sorry flight I'm

_____

6 sir flying us for thank with you

_____

7 day a have good

_____

2 ▶ **Complete the suggestions. Use *I suggest ...* and the correct form of these verbs.**

take ▪ let ▪ visit ▪ have ▪ wear

1 _____ you _____ your coats outside –
Sydney is very hot in December.

2 _____ you _____ the other passengers
get off first.

3 _____ you _____ your passports and
disembarkation forms ready.

4 _____ you _____ a taxi – the shuttle
train is quicker.

5 _____ you _____ the old town – it's
really beautiful.

3 ▶ **Choose the correct options in the purser's final announcement. Listen to audio 10.1 to check your answers.**

Ladies and gentlemen, on [1]*board / behalf* of the captain and the entire crew, we would like to welcome you to Boston, where the [2]*local / latest* time is 14.55.

For your safety, please remain seated with your seatbelt fastened, leaving all items of hand luggage safely [3]*put / stowed*, until the seatbelt signs have been switched [4]*on / off*.

Before you leave the aircraft, please [5]*sure / ensure* you have all your personal items and hand-[6]*luggage / cases* with you. Please be careful when opening overhead lockers as items may fall out causing [7]*injury / problem*.

We would like to [8]*remember / remind* you that smoking is not [9]*permitted / permitting* until you've reached a designated smoking area [10]*upstairs / outside* the terminal building. We would also like to remind all passengers that mobile phones [11]*would / should* not be switched on until the seatbelt signs have been turned [12]*off / on*. ...

We [13]*wish / hope* you a very pleasant stay or a safe [14]*travel / journey* if you are continuing your journey. We hope to see you again in the future. Goodbye.

Taking part in the crew debriefing

4 ▶ **Read this conversation between the captain, the purser and a flight attendant. What was the problem?**

Captain The other incident is more serious. We've all been through training for landing procedures and the safety issues, about making sure everyone knows what is happening between the flight deck and the cabin, so what went wrong?

Purser I think you are referring to the fact that not all the cabin crew were seated in time for landing.

Captain Precisely, in spite of the full sequence of announcements from the flight deck: 20 minutes, ten minutes and even 'Cabin crew, seats for landing'.

Flight attendant This was my fault. I shouldn't have got stuck dealing with that passenger. I didn't check the exit doors in time, and I was late, very late, getting strapped in. I should have acted more quickly.

Purser And that is serious. You should all know that cabin crew must be strapped in for landing.

Captain Listen, I will be reporting on both incidents. Our teamwork was poor and certainly our communication and leadership must be improved.

Purser For me, I'm disappointed. We should all know the procedures, we should all be aware of possible problems and we should all be working for each other all the time.

Captain Exactly. In my report, I'm going to recommend further crew resource management training for all the cabin crew. We've got to do better as a team.

5 Find where the flight attendant uses *should* in the conversation when talking about what happened. Underline four more sentences with *should*.

6 Put the sentences you underlined in exercise 5 in the past tense. Use *should have*.

7 Tick (✓) three things the flight attendant should have done to avoid being late.

1 He should've looked at his watch.
2 He should've checked the exit doors.
3 He should've stopped talking to the passenger.
4 He should've secured the galley.
5 He should've got strapped in.

8 Read the sentences. If they are correct, put a tick (✓). If there are mistakes, correct them.

1 You should sit down now and fasten your seatbelt.
2 You shouldn't to open the overhead lockers now.
3 You should have not got involved in an argument with that passenger.
4 We should do our last checks now.
5 They shouldn't to be going to the toilets any more.
6 We should've told them before.
7 They shouldn't be shouting at all.
8 I should to tell the purser.

9 Complete the crossword.

Across
4 You say this when someone is leaving.
5 'Cabin crew, cabin crew, seats for _____.'
6 Opposite of *quiet*
7 Serious and urgent events
9 Leave the ground
10 'This man is ill – is there a _____ on board?'
11 A meeting where you get information

Down
1 You find this on a menu.
2 You might get a lot of these if the flight is delayed.
3 You say this when you greet passengers.
8 The person in command of an aircraft

LOG BOOK

Think about the disembarkation of passengers.
➤ Are there still safety precautions to tell passengers about?
➤ Do you have the same attitude when you welcome passengers as when you say goodbye to them?
➤ What kinds of things do you say to passengers as they leave the aircraft?

Think about a bad experience you've had as passengers are leaving the aircraft.
➤ What happened? Did you expect it, or was it a surprise?
➤ How did you reply? Did you get angry or discuss things calmly?
➤ What do you say to passengers who are difficult at this time?

Think about crew debriefings.
➤ What is usually discussed? Is it always about something that went wrong? Can you think of examples?
➤ Is this debriefing important for you in your career? How do you assess your performance and progress?

Notes

❝ *Please remain seated until the plane is parked at the gate. At no time in history has a passenger beaten a plane to the gate. So please don't even try.* ❞ Cabin crew member

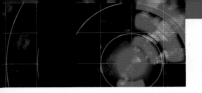

Word list

Unit 1

briefing / pre-briefing *n*
colleague *n*
co-ordination *n*
crew member *n*
duties *n pl*
galley leader *n*
long-haul *adj*
passenger load *n*
procedures *n pl*
purser *n*
schedule *n*
seat configuration *n*
stowage area *n*
turbulence *n*

Multi-word verbs

find out
fly with
look forward to
wait for
work with

Cabin crew personal belongings

carry-on bag *n*
epaulettes *n pl*
flight papers *n pl*
freshener *n*
meals service apron *n*
name tab *n*
operations manual *n*
overnight bag *n*
passport *n*
toilet kit *n*
uniform *n*

Unit 2

aisle seat *n*
baby bassinet *n*
boarding pass *n*
brace position *n*
buckle / unbuckle *v*
carry-on bag *n*
check-in *n*
clip *n*
elastic band *n*
electronic device *n*
emergency exit *n*
entertainment handset *n*
evacuate *v*
extension seatbelt *n*
fasten *v*
floor-level lighting *n*
hand-baggage *n*
life-vest *n*
overhead locker *n*
oxygen mask *n*
safety demonstration *n*
seatbelt *n*
upright *adj*

Multi-word verbs

carry on
go straight across
listen to
pass behind
pull down
put sth over sth
switch off
take out

Passenger seats

arm-rest *n*
call button *n*
foot-rest *n*
handset controls *n pl*
head-rest *n*
light button *n*
seat incline *n*
seat pocket *n*
tray table *n*
window blind *n*

Unit 3

appreciate *v*
arrogant *adj*
call button *n*
call light *n*
cooperation *n*
demanding *adj*
disembarkation card *n*
film channel *n*
headphones *n pl*
headset *n*
menu card *n*
purchases *n pl*
seat pocket *n*
snacks *n pl*
starving *adj*
tight connection *n*
trolley *n*
unpleasant *adj*

Multi-word verbs

ask for
call for
come back
get back to (sb)
move around
plug in
walk around

Passenger types

celebrity *n*
furious *adj*
grumpy *adj*
jolly *adj*
polite *adj*
unfriendly *adj*
VIP *n*

Unit 4

bargain *n*
be designed for *v*
dressing *n*
kosher *adj*
local currency *n*
major credit cards *n pl*
mild *adj*
pre-order *v*
recommend *v*
sauce *n*
special meal *n*
spicy *adj*
take an order *v*
vegetarian *adj*

Multi-word verbs

get sth for sb
pass sth to sb
pay by (card)
pay with (cash)

More food and drink

bagel *n*
brunch *n*
cheese board *n*
self-service snacks *n pl*
smoked salmon starter *n*
sweet and sour *adj*

Unit 5

acclimatize *v*
diplomat *n*
freezing *adj*
handset *n*
nanny *n*
paracetamol *n*
properly *adv*
temperature *n*
transit *n*
troublesome *adj*
video screen *n*
volume button *n*

Multi-word verbs

ask for
check on
go on and off
listen to
run out of
sort out
think about

Passenger problems

a broken reading light
a broken seat
a child kicking your seat
changing seats
inedible food

Unit 6

accident *n*
administer *v*
anticipate *v*
antiseptic wipe *n*
appreciate *v*
bandage *n*
bump *n, v*
cardiac arrest *n*
compress *n*
condition *n*
cut *n, v*
defibrillator *n*
diabetic *adj*
diagnosis *n*
dizzy *adj*
dressing *n*
faint *v*
first aid *n*
incident *n*
inconvenience *n*
indigestion *n*

injection *n*
injury *n*
medication *n*
pain *n*
pulse *n*
unconscious *adj*
wound *n*

Multi-word verbs

care for
give to
hand over
look after
put in
take care of

Sick passengers

collapse *v*
diarrhoea *n*
dizziness *n*
fit of coughing *n*
headache *n*
stomach pain *n*
vomiting *n*

Unit 7

abort *v*
aware *adj*
belongings *n pl*
bird strike *n*
briefcase *n*
cabin pressure *n*
calm *adj*
ditch *v*
escape route *n*
float *v*
grab *v*
high-heeled shoes *n pl*
hyperventilate *v*
locate *v*
loss *n*
massive *adj*
Mayday *n*
miracle *n*
nausea *n*
PAN-PAN *n*
relax *v*
submerge *v*
technical *adj*
upper deck *n*

Multi-word verbs

pull down
put sth over sth
stay in (your seats)

Emergencies

decompression *n*
engine failure *n*
human error *n*
loss of control *n*
mechanical failure *n*
sudden descent *n*

Unit 8

aggressive *adj*
apologize *v*
arrest *v*
awful *adj*
dirty *adj*
disgusting *adj*
disruptive *adj*
disturb *v*
favour *n*
handcuff *v*
jetty *n*
official *adj*
patient *adj*
reassure *v*
restrain *v*
restraining straps *n pl*
sort out *v*
state (of sth) *n*
unruly *adj*
vacant *adj*

Multi-word verbs

ask for
care about
come over
go over
sort out
turn down
turn up
warm up

Complaints

cabin temperature *n*
food quality *n*
in-flight service delays *n pl*

lack of information *n*
seating arrangements *n pl*
waiting time *n*

Unit 9

all clear *n, adj*
approximately *adj*
bang *v*
bar seals *n pl*
bother *v*
clear *v*
clear in *v*
climb *v*
connection *n*
customs *n pl*
descend *v*
detach *v*
domestic terminal *n*
ensure *v*
final warning *n*
flight deck *n*
galley *n*
immigration *n*
in transit *adj*
in-seat power *n*
minibus *n*
onward journey *n*
overhead bins *n pl*
paperwork *n*
rubbish *n*
secure *v*
store *v*
stress *n, v*
warn *v*
window blind *n*

Multi-word verbs

bang on
bring upright
clear in
fold away
put away
put in
put under
put up
speed up
strap in
switch off

Last-minute checks

children's seat belts *n pl*
exit rows *n pl*
passenger debris *n*
secure galley *v*
tray tables *n pl*

Unit 10

assumption *n*
cause *v*
communication *n*
company policy *n*
crew coordination *n*
customer care *n*
debriefing *n*
decision-making *n*
designated area *n*
essential *adj*
ongoing *adj*
precisely *adv*
problem-solving *n*
promptly *adv*
review *n, v*
safety issues *n pl*
shut-down *n*
speed up *v*
spillage *n*
stowed *adj*
teamwork *n*
urgency *n*
valuable lesson *n*
vital *adj*

Multi-word verbs

check on
shut down
sit down
stand up
switch on
take away
talk about

Leaving the plane

aft left-hand door *n*
airbridge *n*
forward left-hand door *n*
gate *n*
mobile steps *n pl*
mobility equipment *n*
row by row *adv*

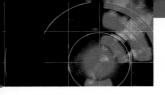

Glossary of key expressions

Unit 1

Introducing yourself to someone you do not know

My name's Paola. Pleased to meet you.
Hi there, I'm Tom.

Finding out someone's name

Sorry, what's your name?
Excuse me, could tell me your name, please?

Introducing other people

This is my colleague, Katrin.
This is Hemal.

Saying hello to people you know or have met before

Hello again, how are you?   Fine thanks. And you?
How's it going?   Very well, thanks.
How are you?   Not too bad.
Hi there!   Hi!

Checking and clarifying

Can I just check what the flight time is?
Can you confirm that your crew is familiar with the cockpit procedures?
Can I clarify something?
Can I clarify the time of the meals service?

Unit 2

Polite requests

Can I see your boarding pass?
Can I look at your seat number, please?
Could I please see your boarding pass?
Could I check your seat number, please?
Please can I check the seating arrangements?
Please would you sit here for the moment?
Would you follow me, please?
Would you please turn off your mobile phone?
Would you mind just taking this seat until I have checked the passenger list?
Welcome aboard.
Good morning.
Good afternoon.
Good evening.
Hello, how are you?
Hello there, how are you today?

Can I help you, madam?
Can I help you, sir?
This way, please.
Here you are.
Straight across the cabin and turn left.
That's right.
Carry on down the cabin.

Showing how something works

Can you show me how it works?
Of course. / Certainly.
This is how it works.
First of all, you … .
Then you … and … .
Is that OK / all right with you?

Unit 3

Dealing with passenger needs

Can I help you?
What can I do for you?
How can I help?
Let me help you.
I'll find out for you.
Let me explain.
What's the problem?

Asking passengers politely to wait

I'm afraid we're busy just now. Can you wait a moment?
Can you wait until we've finished the service?
Leave it with me and I'll do it as soon as possible.
I'll get back to you, I promise.

Being attentive and caring to passengers

Hello, madam, are you feeling better now?
Can I help you, sir?
Did you call, sir?
Hello there, is everything all right?
No problem, madam.
I do apologize. I'll get it immediately.
You are quite right, sir.
Yes, that's fine. Go ahead.

'Comfort' expressions

Here you are.
Can I get you anything else?
Anything else I can do for you?
Let me put the call light on (for you).
Don't worry, you'll be fine.
Of course, no problem at all.
I'll be back in five minutes.

Unit 4

Offering a choice

What would you like, sir?
What would you like to drink?
What can I get you, madam?
Here we are, sir.
There you are, madam.

Money transactions

The perfume costs 41 dollars.
The scarves are 72 dollars each.
Forty-one plus [+] 72 makes 113 dollars.
Four times [x] eight equals [=] 32 dollars.
A hundred dollars minus [−] 85 – that's 15 dollars change.
That comes to 120 euros.
How will you be paying? By card or with cash?
How would you like to pay?
Here's your receipt, your card and your gifts.

Unit 5

Finding out the problem

Did you call, sir?
What's the problem?
What's the matter?
How can I help (you)?

Offering to help (1)

I'll check on our arrival time and get back to you.
I'll ask if there is a doctor or nurse on board.
I'll get you a blanket.
I'll get it now.
I'll show you how it works.
I'll get you another one.

Apologizing

Sorry, we don't have any peppermint – my mistake.

I'm afraid we've only got apple juice and orange juice today.

I do apologize.

I am sorry, but we've run out of cheese.

I can only apologize, sir.

Sorry about that.

I'm really sorry, we haven't got any left.

Unit 6

Check ➤ Call ➤ Care

Check

Do you have any pain?

Do you feel well enough to sit up?

How are you feeling?

Call

I need some help.

Get the first aid kit immediately.

Can you get her a glass of water, please?

Care

I'm going to clean up the wound and put a dressing over it.

Can you hold this compress against your forehead?

Giving instructions to crew

Bilal, grab the oxygen.

Get Safiya to call Anton.

Help me get the mask over his head.

Tell the captain.

Make an announcement immediately.

Talking about the past

What happened?

What was the problem?

What did you do?

Was there a doctor on board?

Unit 7

Giving instructions

Stay in your seats.

Remain calm.

Pull down the oxygen mask.

Pull it down over your nose and mouth.

Breathe normally.

Please keep quiet.

Don't worry, you'll be fine.

Listen, stop.

Don't be upset. We'll take care of her.

Keep quiet please – you are disturbing others.

Don't shout, speak normally.

Breathe slowly and deeply. That's it.

Calm down now, please.

That's enough – control yourself.

Try to relax. I'll stay with you.

Listen carefully please, these instructions are for you.

Wait until we land.

Instructions not to do something

Do not leave your seats until instructed to do so by your crew.

Do not / Don't take anything with you as you leave the aircraft.

Do not / Don't take handbags or briefcases.

Unit 8

Offering to help (2)

Let me just check the special meals list.

Let me get an official form for you.

Let me see if I can get you another one.

Let me get you a blanket.

If ...

If the situation doesn't get better, then I'll try to find you another seat.

If there's still a problem, then I'll come over.

If there is still a problem, I won't leave you on your own.

I'll get you another drink if you keep your voices down.

Special requests

Could I ask you a special favour?

Would you mind just keeping the noise down a little?

Please could you come over to help me?

Expressing obligation

I have to speak to the captain.

I've got to speak to the captain.

I must speak to the captain.

We must call the police / security.

We need to call the police / security.

You have to sit down, sir.

You have to stop that now.

You have to be quiet.

You have to do what the captain says.

Unit 9

Word order in multi-word verbs

Put away the case.   Put it away.

Turn / Switch off your electronic devices.   Turn / Switch them off.

Fold away your table.   Fold it away.

Turn up / down the heating.   Turn it up / down.

Put your seat back upright.   Put it upright.

Put your bags in the locker.   Put them in the locker.

Talking about time

What time / When does the flight land / take off?

It lands / takes off at 10.15.

What time / When is the flight?

At 10.15.

How long does it take to get / go to the domestic terminal?

It takes about five minutes.

How long is the flight?

About two hours.

Checking things have been done

Have you done all the checks?

Yes, I've completed all the checks. / Yes, I have.

Have you done all the clearing in?

No, I haven't cleared in all the rows yet. / No, I haven't.

Has she finished the bar paperwork?

Yes, she has. / No, she hasn't.

Has she done the final checks?

No, she hasn't.

Have you secured the trolley in the galley?

Yes, I have.

Have they checked the tables are upright?

No, they haven't.

Have we done everything?

Yes, we have.

Unit 10

Making a recommendation

I suggest (that) you have your coats ready.
I suggest (that) you take the airport bus.
I suggest (that) you don't get up immediately.

Saying goodbye

Thank you for flying with us, sir.
Goodbye, madam.
Have a good holiday.
Enjoy your trip.
Look forward to seeing you again soon.
Have a good day, Mr Gerighty.

should

We should talk about two incidents now.
You should act more promptly in future.
You shouldn't continue serving food next time.
You should've shut down the service immediately.
You should've told them to stop.
I should've communicated better.
We shouldn't have been late.

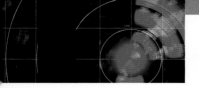

Audio scripts

Unit 1

 1.1

Paola Hi. Are you on the flight to Boston at 10.20?

Tom Yes, I am. Are you on the same flight?

Paola Yeah! My name's Paola, by the way.

Tom Hi, Paola. I'm Tom. It's nice to meet you.

Jenny Hello, Paola, I'm Jenny.

Paola Hi, Jenny. It's nice to meet you.

Jenny Sorry, what's your name?

Tom My name's Tomasz, but I prefer to be called Tom. Anyway, pleased to meet you, Jenny.

Jenny I'm sure I've flown with you before, Paola, but I can't remember what trip we did together.

Paola Yes, I feel I know you, too!

Tom We'd better go now, the shuttle is waiting and our briefing starts in ten minutes.

1.2

Tom Good morning, Katrin. How are you today?

Katrin Fine thanks, Tom. How about you? Have you had some good trips recently?

Tom Yes, I had a great roster last month! And I've just got back from a 4-day Hongkong trip. The flight was really busy, but I had a fantastic team! Are you looking forward to going to Boston?

Katrin Definitely. The shops are fantastic there! Mind you, I was in a bit of a panic last night – I couldn't find my passport! It took me ages to find it! I thought I was going to have to come off this flight.

Tom I'm glad you found it! I was looking forward to working with you again as it's my first trip to Boston. By the way, this is Paola.

Paola Oh, we've met before! Hello, Katrin, how are you?

Katrin Very well, thanks. It's nice to see you again.

Paola This is Jenny.

Katrin Hi, Jenny.

Jenny Hi there, Katrin. *[Pause]* Paola, I've just remembered which trip we did together! It was to Madrid back in June.

Paola Oh, that's right! How could I forget! It was a really turbulent flight, wasn't it! Didn't you drop a full drinks tray on that very smartly dressed businessman and he went a bit crazy?

Jenny Wow! Yes! You have a good memory. Anyway, how are you?

Paola Not too bad now. I've been off sick for a week, so it's great to be back flying. In fact, I think you and Tom are part of my team today.

1.3

Ted Good morning everyone, and welcome to DZ107 flight to Boston. For those who haven't flown with me before, my name's Ted. I'm your purser in charge of today's flight. I'd also like to introduce you to your cabin supervisors: Katrin Larsson is going to be in charge of Business today and Leila Ahmed is in charge of Economy.

Katrin Hello, everyone.

Leila Hi, everyone. It's nice to see some new and familiar faces.

Ted Can I just check that everyone has got their working positions and door responsibilities?

All crew Yes.

Ted And I see we have a new long-haul crew member joining us today – Jutta Weber. Welcome to long-haul, Jutta. You'll be working with Leila and Hemal, so if you're unsure of any of your responsibilities, I'm sure they'll be glad to help you out.

Jutta Thanks. I'm really excited about my first long-haul flight!

Leila Hi, Jutta, I'm Leila, the FA7 galley leader. I'll be sitting at Door 4 Left, working with you and Hemal. When we get on board, if you need any help with your pre-take-off duties or stowage areas, just let us know.

Jutta Thank you very much.

Ted OK. Before I give you any flight details …

1.4

My name's Paola. Pleased to meet you.
Hi there, I'm Tom.
Sorry, what's your name?
Excuse me, could tell me your name, please?
This is my colleague, Katrin.
This is Hemal.
Hello again, how are you?   Fine thanks.
                                         And you?
How's it going?   Very well, thanks.
How are you?   Not too bad.
Hi there!   Hi!

1.5

Captain Good morning, everyone. My name is Kurt Ostermeier and I'm your captain today. This is my first officer, Rick Schultz. You'll be pleased to hear that we've got a really quick flight time today of nine hours 20 minutes and, apparently, the weather in Boston is good, but cold. Rick, you wanted a word about the weather during the flight.

First officer Yes, thanks. I just wanted to warn the crew of some moderate turbulence during flight – this is due to strong winds and storms over the Atlantic. We anticipate this turbulence about 3½ hours into the flight.

Ted Oh, right! The main cabin service should be over by then.

First officer Good. We'll try to give you as much warning as possible and it may be necessary for the crew to be seated and strapped in during the worst of it.

Ted Thanks, Rick – we'll try to get the drinks and meal service finished early, then.

Leila Excuse me, can I clarify something?

Ted Sure.

Leila Can we delay the main meal service until the turbulence is over?

Ted No, sorry, we'll have to follow normal procedure. You can never schedule the weather.

Captain Ted, can you confirm that your crew is familiar with the cockpit procedures?

Ted Yes, Captain. All crew members are familiar with the rules and procedures regarding the cockpit.

Captain Great. OK then. Let's go and have a good flight!

 1.6

Can I just check what the flight time is?
Can you confirm that your crew is familiar with the cockpit procedures?
Can I clarify something?
Can I clarify the time of the meals service?

Unit 2

 2.1

Jenny Good morning, madam. Welcome on board.

Woman Thanks.

Jenny Can I see your boarding pass, please?

Woman Yes ... here you are.

Jenny 27G ... go straight across to the other side, and then turn right. You'll see the seat numbers on the overhead lockers. My colleague will show you where your seat is.

Woman Thank you.

Jenny Hello, madam. Welcome on board ... you're together? Turn right here, go straight down the cabin past the toilets. You'll find your seats at the front of the next cabin, in the middle section. ... Hello, how are you today, sir? May I check your boarding pass ...

 2.2

Jenny Can I help you, madam? Seat number 17D. Yes, come this way. Yours is the aisle seat just here.

Woman An aisle seat? I specifically asked for a window seat.

Jenny Did you? I *am* sorry. You've been given an aisle seat. Did you request a window seat at check-in?

Woman Yes ... and I told her I can't fly if I can't have a seat by the window. She assured me I had a window seat.

Jenny Oh dear, I'm really sorry about this. But don't worry – the flight isn't full today and I'm sure I can sort out a window seat for you. Would you mind just taking this seat until I have checked the passenger list? It will only take a couple of minutes.

Woman Are you sure? I don't want to stay here for the flight.

Jenny Don't worry, I'll be back in a moment with a better seat for you, madam.

 2.3

1 Welcome on board.
2 Good morning.
3 Good afternoon.
4 Good evening.
5 Hello, how are you?
6 Hello there, how are you today?
7 Could I please see your boarding pass?
8 Would you mind just taking this seat until I have checked the passenger list?
9 Can I help you, madam?
10 Can I help you, sir?
11 Would you follow me, please?
12 This way, please.
13 Here you are.
14 Straight across the cabin and turn left.
15 That's right.
16 Carry on down the cabin.

 2.4

Sylvie Everything all right, Jenny?

Jenny Yes, fine. Nearly all the passengers are on board now ... Hello sir, you're in row 11. Let me see, madam. Yes, this way, on the left, 8D – it's the aisle seat.

Jenny I need a window seat for a passenger. Do you have the Passenger List?

Sylvie Yes, I've got it – here, have a look.

Jenny Great – there's a window seat free in 15A, Sylvie. Would you mind if I gave 15A to my passenger?

Sylvie No problem, Jenny. You go ahead. I'll carry on greeting the remaining passengers ... Hello. Welcome on board. Are you together?

Passengers Yes.

Jenny Hello, madam. I've got a window seat for you in 15A – it's just a couple rows in front. Would that be OK for you?

Woman Any window seat will be fine, thanks.

Jenny Do you need any help with your bags?

Woman Oh, thank you – you could take this for me ...

Jenny Follow me.

Woman Many thanks, I really appreciate this.

Jenny No problem at all. My name's Jenny. If you need anything during the flight, I'll be happy to help you. I hope you enjoy your flight.

Woman Many thanks, Jenny.

2.5

Sylvie Jenny, Mrs Lenchik will need a bassinet for her baby after take-off. Can I leave you to look after her?

Jenny Certainly. Welcome on board, Mrs Lenchik. My name is Jenny and I'll be looking after you during your flight. How old is your baby?

Woman She'll be 11 months tomorrow!

Jenny Ah, she's asleep! She's beautiful. Has she flown before?

Woman No. This is my first flight with her. Actually, I've only just managed to get her to sleep – she's been a bit difficult in the departure lounge. I'm hoping she'll stay asleep during take-off.

Jenny OK. Your baby will need to be seated on your lap for take-off and landing, fastened to your seatbelt with a special baby belt. It's just like an extension seatbelt. Hopefully we won't wake her up! I'll go and get one for you and show you how it works. After take-off, I'll bring you a bassinet cot for your baby ... and if you need anything during the flight, just let me know. I'll be back with the baby belt in just a minute, OK?

Woman Thanks.

 2.6

Sylvie Hello, sir. Welcome on board. May I see your boarding pass, please?

Man Yes ... sorry I'm late. I was delayed getting from the city to the airport.

Sylvie No problem. We've been expecting you ... 4F – cross to the other side and turn left.

Man Many thanks.

Sylvie Jenny, that's it, everyone is on board. Can you check the doors? *[on the interphone]* Tom, doors check, please. OK, prepare for the safety demo.

Jenny OK. Zone C cabin secure.

Tom OK. Zone D and E cabin secure ...

2.7

Ladies and gentlemen, even if you are a frequent traveller, it is important that you listen carefully to the following safety instructions.

You will find a safety instruction card in the pocket in front of you. Please read this carefully before take-off and familiarize yourself with the emergency exits and procedures on board this Boeing 777S.

When the seatbelt sign is on, you must fasten your seatbelt. To do this, insert the metal fitting into the buckle – like this – and tighten by pulling the strap – like this. To undo the seatbelt, lift the buckle – like this.

We suggest you keep the seatbelt fastened throughout the flight.

There are several emergency exits on this aircraft. They are being pointed out to you now. Please take a few moments now to locate your nearest exit. It may be behind you. If you are sitting in an emergency exit, you must know how to open the door in an emergency and when instructed to do so by the crew.

If we need to evacuate the aircraft, floor level lighting will guide you to the exits.

In the event of an emergency landing, you will hear 'Brace, brace' and you must adopt this position. Look at the card for the brace position.

Your life vest is under your seat. This is how you put it on.

First, take it out of the pouch and put it over your head. Then pass the straps around your waist and tie them in front. Do not inflate the vest until you leave the aircraft. To inflate the vest, pull on this red cord. Use the whistle and light to attract attention.

If the pressure drops, an oxygen mask will automatically drop from the compartment above your head. To start the flow of oxygen, pull the mask towards you, put it firmly over your mouth and nose and secure the elastic band behind your head and breathe normally. If you are travelling with a child or a person who needs assistance, put your mask on first and then assist the other person.

Finally, make sure your seat backs are upright, your tables are folded away and your hand-baggage is either in the overhead locker or under the seat in front of you.

All electronic devices must now be switched off for take-off.

We wish you all an enjoyable flight.

 2.8

1 Hello there, this is the exit row. Have you read the safety instructions card carefully? *[Pause]* Good. Thanks for that.

2 Can you put your table up, please, before take-off?

3 Sorry, you'll have to switch your computer off during take-off.

4 Is your child's seatbelt fastened securely, madam?

5 Hello sir, this is an emergency exit, so no bags are allowed on the floor. Would you mind putting your bag in the overhead locker for take-off?

6 Sorry, you'll have to switch off your mobile now.

7 Could you put your seat in the upright position, please?

8 Sir, we're preparing for take-off, so can you fasten your seatbelt, please?

Unit 3

3.1

1 Ladies and gentlemen, boys and girls, it's great to have you on board. The seat-belt sign is off, but please don't leave your seats unless you have to. This is only a short flight and we'd like to serve you drinks and snacks as quickly as possible. There will only be time for one service and, er ... apologies, we don't have any hot snacks today. Sorry about that. Speak to you again soon.

2 Hello everyone, this is Stefan speaking. The seat-belt sign is off. Feel free to walk around. We want to serve you drinks shortly, so watch out for the trolley – we don't want to run you down, so don't block the aisles. We don't have a lot of time, so be ready with your order please, and your money, of course. Thanks for your cooperation. Have a good flight.

3 Ladies and gentlemen, the seat-belt sign has been switched off and you can move around the cabin. We shall be coming through the cabin with refreshments in a few moments. Kindly look at the menu card in the pocket in front of you and have your orders ready, please. We'd really appreciate it if you had the exact change for your purchases. Thank you, and enjoy the flight.

3.2

1 It's great to have you on board.

2 Please don't leave your seats unless you have to.

3 We'd like to serve you drinks and snacks as quickly as possible.

4 The seatbelt sign is off.

5 Feel free to walk around.

6 Thanks for your cooperation.

7 We shall be coming through the cabin with refreshments in a few moments.

8 We'd really appreciate it if you had the exact change for your purchases.

3.3

1

FA Excuse me, excuse me, could you sit down, please? We need to get past with the trolley. We don't have a lot of time.

Man Listen, I'm sorry, but I have to go to the toilet.

FA OK, no problem. Sorry about that.

2

Woman Sorry to bother you, can I have a glass of water? I have to take my medicine.

FA Yes, of course. We're coming through the cabin now and I'll bring it to you. What seat are you in?

Woman 11D. Thanks.

3

FA Hello, can I help you?

Woman Yes, could you heat my baby's bottle, please?

FA I'm afraid we're busy just now. Can you wait a moment?

Woman Not really. I have to feed her now. She's been crying for a long time.

FA Leave it with me and I'll do it as soon as possible.

Woman Many thanks.

4

Man Excuse me.

FA What can I do for you?

Man Erm ... on arrival I have to get from Terminal 2 to Terminal 3. How long will it take? I've got a pretty tight connection.

FA Ah, yes. Look, we have to start the refreshments service now. Can you wait until we've finished the service, and then I'll explain everything for you?

Man OK, but can I remind you in about 30 minutes? I'm really nervous about missing the next flight.

FA Listen, don't worry. I'll get back to you. I promise.

Man Thanks.

3.4

Can I help you?
What can I do for you?
Yes, of course.
OK, no problem.

I'm afraid we're busy just now. Can you wait a moment?
Can you wait until we've finished the service?
Leave it with me and I'll do it as soon as possible.
I'll get back to you. I promise.

3.5

1

FA Hello, madam, are you feeling better now?

Woman Yes, thank you. But I can't get my bag down from the overhead locker.

FA Let me help.

Woman Thank you so much

FA No problem, madam. My pleasure.

2

FA Can I help you, sir?

Man Yes, you can. I asked for a blanket ten minutes ago.

FA Ah yes, I do apologize. I'll get it immediately.

3

FA Did you call, sir?

Man Yes, several times. In fact, I don't understand. You announced the meals service a long time ago. When are you going to serve us? It's really poor.

FA You're quite right, sir, but good news – we're just about to start the meals service.

4

FA Hello there, is everything all right?

Woman Can I change my seat, please? There's an empty seat over there.

FA You're right. Let me just quickly check the passenger list to make sure it's empty. *[Pause]* Yes, that's fine. Go ahead.

Woman Thanks very much.

3.6

Hello, madam, are you feeling better now?
Can I help you, sir?
Did you call, sir?
Hello there, is everything all right?
No problem, madam.
I do apologize. I'll get it immediately.
You're quite right, sir.
Yes, that's fine. Go ahead.

3.7

1

FA Here's the menu, sir.

Man Oh, thank you. By the way, how long is the flight?

FA Eleven hours.

Man But the captain said we arrive at 14.45.

FA That's local time.

Man Oh, of course.

FA Anything else I can do for you?

Man No thanks, I'm fine.

2

FA Menu? ... Menu? Here you are, madam.

Woman Ah good, will you be serving the meals soon?

FA Well, there'll be drinks first and then the meal will follow.

Woman So ... in about one hour?

FA A little earlier, I think. It's ten o'clock now, so let's say about 10.45.

Woman That's good, my two boys are starving.

FA Really! Let me try to find something when I come back with the drinks shortly.

Woman That would be very kind. Thanks.

3

FA Headphones, madam?

Woman Thanks. Can the girls have them as well?

FA Of course. Have they used them before?

Woman Yes, they showed *me* how to use them. And the handsets!

FA Ah, good. Films are on Channel 2, girls, OK?

4

FA Headphones, sir?

Man Thanks. Oh, can I have a blanket, please?

FA Sure. Are you cold?

Man Just a little, but I'm not complaining.

FA I'll bring it to you in a moment. Let me put the call light on to remind me. Can I get you anything else, sir?

Man No, that's fine, thank you very much.

3.8

Here you are.
Can I get you anything else?
Anything else I can do for you?
Let me put the call light on (for you).
Don't worry, you'll be fine.
Of course, no problem at all.
I'll be back in five minutes.

Unit 4

 4.1

FA   Would you like beef or chicken, sir? Or the vegetarian option, the lasagne?
Man   Beef, please.
FA   Here we are. What would you like to drink?
Man   A glass of red wine, please.
FA   OK.
Man   Is it French?
FA   No, it's a South African wine – it's very nice – would you like to try it?
Man   Yes. Thanks.
FA   And you, madam, would you like beef or chicken or the lasagne?
Woman   Oh, have you got any fish?
FA   No, I'm sorry. Our choices are beef, chicken or vegetable lasagne today.
Woman   Is the chicken very spicy?
FA   No, it's just mildly spiced – it's not like a curry – would you like to try it?
Woman   Good, I'll take the chicken. Could I have a glass of water too, please?
FA   Certainly, madam. Would you like still or sparkling?
Woman   Still, please.
FA   There you are. Enjoy your meal ... and what about your children?
Woman   Do you have children's meals on board?
FA   We do carry pre-ordered special children's meals for passengers who have booked prior to their flight. Did you book them?
Woman   No, I'm afraid I didn't.
FA   Well, I could check to see if we have any spare meals for you. Would you like me to do that?
Woman   Oh, yes, please. That would be great.

FA   I'll be back in a moment. *[Pause]* I've got two children's meals here that have been ordered, but not needed! It's burger and chips and fun food they'll really enjoy! Would they like these?
Woman   Oh – it's their favourite food! Thank you so much!
FA   You're very welcome. There you are. Would you like a drink with your meal, boys?
Woman   They'd like a 7up with no ice, please.
FA   If you're returning with us, it might be possible to order your children a special child's meal for their flight home. I can come back to you after the meals service and discuss if you'd like?
Woman   That would be great, thanks.
FA   No problem. I'll be back after the meals service then. Enjoy your meal! Would you like chicken or beef sir? ...

 4.2

Coffee or tea?
Red or white wine?
Still or sparkling?
Beef or chicken?
Brown or white?
Vegetarian or non-vegetarian?

 4.3

soda
Perrier
apple juice
Sauvignon Blanc
Johnny Walker
Merlot
cognac
fruit tea
Bloody Mary
hot chocolate
vodka
Martini
Kronenberg
Bacardi rum
cappuccino
diet Coke
lemonade
bottled still water
port
Carlsberg
Bordeaux
champagne

tomato juice
tonic water
Earl Grey tea
ginger ale
bourbon
English Breakfast tea
espresso

 4.4

1
FA   What would you like to drink?
Woman   A large glass of water, first of all, and a gin and tonic, please.
FA   No problem. Ice with your water?
Woman   No, thanks.
2
FA   What can I get you, sir?
Man   What kind of fruit juice have you got?
FA   Apple, orange, pineapple or tomato.
Man   Pineapple, please.
3
FA   What would you like, sir?
Man   Could I have a cup of tea, please?
FA   Yes, of course. Do you mind waiting a moment? We're serving cold drinks just now.
Man   Oh sorry, I'll have an apple juice then, and the tea later.
FA   Are you sure?
Man   Yes, that'll be fine.
4
FA   Would you like a drink from the bar, sir?
Man   Do you have a cold beer?
FA   Sure, Heineken or a local beer?
Man   I'll try a local one, please.
FA   Here you are.
5
Child   Can we have two large glasses of Coke, please?
FA   With ice, I guess.
Child   Yes, please.
FA   Here we are. Enjoy.
6
Woman   Excuse me, could I have another glass of white wine?
FA   By all means. Pass your glass, please. There you are.
Woman   Many thanks. The meal is great, by the way.
FA   Glad you're enjoying it.

7

Man Excuse me, I'd like another vodka.
FA Sorry sir, we'll be landing in 30 minutes and the drinks bar has been closed. Can I get you a soft drink, perhaps?
Man No, thanks.

4.5

Apple, orange, pineapple or tomato.
Coke, Fanta, Sprite, 7up or Lilt.
Red wine, white wine, sherry or champagne.
Earl Grey, English Breakfast, peppermint or green.
Still water, sparkling water, soda water or tonic water.
Espresso, cappucino, decaffeinated or regular.

4.6

Ladies and gentlemen, the duty-free sales will begin shortly. Please prepare your list of purchases. Check the *Shopping on Board* magazine in your seat pocket. All prices are in local currency and in US dollars, and you can pay by cash or by using a credit card. We accept most major credit cards. Frequent flyers win points on all sales on board. There are some excellent bargains and there are several items specially designed for our airline.

4.7

FA Perfumes, gifts, chocolates, alcohol, toys ...
Man Yes, please.
FA What can I get for you, sir?
Man I'm looking for a light perfume for my daughter's birthday.
FA I have the perfect one, no ... two. Both are 100 mls. This one is delightful, and it's a bargain at only 41 dollars. The other one is a classic – the very best, but more expensive at 65 dollars.
Man Which one do you recommend?
FA I really like this one.
Man And it costs 41 dollars?
FA Yes, that's right.
Man OK, I'll take it.
FA How would you like to pay?

Man By credit card. But just a minute, can I also see the airline's specially designed scarves?
FA Of course. They're pure silk and they're ... let me see, 72 dollars each.
Man I'll take one.
FA So that comes to – let me add it up ... 41 plus 72 ... 113 dollars.
Man OK. Here's my credit card and my frequent flyers card, too, for the points.
FA Thank you. Would you like a receipt, or just the credit card print-out?
Man I need the receipt too, please.
FA No problem. Here's your receipt, here are your cards and these are your gifts.
Man Many thanks.
FA It's a pleasure. ... Duty Free sales ... yes? ... no? ... *[fade]*

4.8

The perfume costs 41 dollars.
The scarves are 72 dollars each.
Forty-one plus 72 makes 113 dollars.
Four times eight equals 32 dollars.
A hundred dollars minus 85 – that's 15 dollars change.
That comes to 120 euros.
How will you be paying? By card or with cash?
How would you like to pay?
Here's your receipt, your card and your gifts.

Unit 5

5.1

FA Did you call, sir?
Man Ah yes, I don't understand this thing.
FA Your handset?
Man Yes.
FA What's the problem?
Man I don't have any sound, I'm afraid.
FA Oh, I'm sorry about that. Have you checked your headphones are plugged in properly?
Man Yes, it's just that they're not working.

FA Let's see – press the volume button here ... that's right ... and then the up and down button.
Man Ah, that's it. Got it. Many thanks.
FA You're welcome.
Woman Excuse me, I need your help, too.
FA Of course. How can I help? What's the matter?
Woman I can't get the film I want.
FA I'll show you. Press 'Menu' first, then 'Movies'. OK? Which film do you want to see?
Woman This one – *The English Patient*.
FA OK, so press 'Select', and then 'Play', and off you go. Enjoy the film.
Woman Thanks very much.
FA My pleasure.

5.2

1 Did you call, sir?
2 Your handset?
3 OK?
4 What's the problem?
5 What's the matter?
6 How can I help?

5.3

1
Woman Sorry to bother you. I have a short transit time on arrival and this flight was delayed. I'm worried that ...
FA ... you'll miss your connection.
Woman Exactly!
2
Man Excuse me, is it possible to get a snack during the night? I'm already hungry.
FA Of course, we have a self-service in the galley, or you can call.
3
FA You called, madam?
Woman Yes, I certainly did. I told your colleague it was too cold at least 15 minutes ago and, it's still like an ice box.
4
FA Hello, what can I do for you?
Woman My daughter isn't well. I think she's got a high temperature. Do you have any paracetamol?

5.4

1

Woman Sorry to bother you. I have a short transit time on arrival and this flight was delayed. I'm worried that …

FA … you'll miss your connection.

Woman Exactly!

FA Did you check your baggage right through?

Woman Yes.

FA Then you should be OK, so don't worry. I'll check on our arrival time and get back to you.

Woman Thanks for your help.

2

Man Excuse me, is it possible to get a snack during the night? I'm already hungry.

FA Of course, we have a self-service in the galley, or you can call.

Man Fantastic. Maybe I'll have one now before I go to sleep.

FA I'll get it for you. A sandwich or pot noodles?

Man Definitely not pot noodles. A sandwich then. Thanks very much.

FA Don't mention it. I'll get it now.

3

FA You called, madam?

Woman Yes, I certainly did. I told your colleague it was too cold at least 15 minutes ago and, it's still like an ice box.

FA You're right, it is cold. I'm afraid it often takes about 20 minutes for the cabin to acclimatize after take-off. I'll get you a blanket in the meantime, if you'd like.

Woman Oh yes, please. What a good idea!

FA I'll be back in a moment.

4

FA Hello, what can I do for you?

Woman My daughter isn't well. I think she's got a high temperature. Do you have any paracetamol?

FA Yes, but I'm afraid we can't give it, we need a doctor or a nurse. Was she like this before boarding?

Woman No, not at all, she was fine, but she's very hot now and complaining of a bad headache.

FA I'll see what I can do. Oh, how old is she?

Woman Seven.

FA I'll ask if there is a doctor or nurse on board.

 5.5

I'll check on our arrival time and get back to you.

I'll ask if there is a doctor or nurse on board.

I'll get you a blanket.

I'll get it for you.

I'll get it now.

I'll show you how it works.

I'll get you another one.

 5.6

FA What would you like, madam?

Woman 1 Just a cup of tea, please.

FA No problem.

Woman 1 What kind of tea have you got?

FA Er … let me see – Earl Grey and herbal, English Breakfast, peppermint …

Woman 1 Peppermint, yes, so two peppermint teas, please.

FA [slight pause] Oops! Sorry, we don't have any peppermint – my mistake.

Woman 1 Then two Earl Grey.

FA And you, sir. What would you like?

Man 1 A tomato juice, please.

FA I'm afraid we've only got apple juice and orange juice today.

Man 1 Oh, OK, but what a pity. Orange, please.

FA Here you are. I do apologize.

Man 1 Thanks.

FA What can I get you, sir?

Man 2 Two cheese sandwiches, and two diet Cokes, please.

FA Oh dear, I *am* sorry, but we've run out of cheese. They've been very popular today. But I can offer you chicken sandwiches.

Man 2 I don't believe it – it's the same old story. You always seem to run out.

FA Once again, I can only apologize, sir. Would you like the chicken?

Man 2 No way, no thank you.

FA Sorry about that … Madam?

Woman 2 A peppermint tea, please.

FA I'm really sorry, we haven't got any left. We've got Earl Grey.

 5.7

FA What can I get you, sir?

Man Two cheese sandwiches and two diet Cokes, please.

FA Oh dear, I *am* sorry, but we've run out of cheese. They've been very popular today. But I can offer you chicken sandwiches.

Man I don't believe it – it's the same old story. You always seem to run out.

FA Once again, I can only apologize, sir. Would you like the chicken?

Man No way, no thank you.

FA Sorry about that.

 5.8

Sorry, we don't have any peppermint – my mistake.

I'm afraid we've only got apple juice and orange juice today.

I do apologize.

I am sorry, but we've run out of cheese.

I can only apologize, sir.

Sorry about that.

I'm really sorry, we haven't got any left.

UNIT 6

 6.1

Ted Ladies and gentlemen. The captain has switched on the seatbelt sign. Please return immediately to your seats and fasten your seatbelts. Due to air turbulence, all in-flight service is suspended and will be resumed as soon as possible.

Leila Hemal, can you bring your trolley back to the galley as quickly as possible and get it stowed away securely?

Hemal Yes … but those people in row 20 haven't sat down yet …

Leila What are they doing still standing around! OK, I'll deal with that. [Pause] … Excuse me, can you sit down and fasten your seatbelts please? [Pause]

Man This lady's been hurt. She's bleeding.

Leila What's happened? [speaks to injured passenger] Hello … are you all right? Can you hear me?

Man   The overhead locker flew open with the turbulence and a laptop fell onto her head. I think she's unconscious!

Leila   OK, thank you for letting me know. I'll deal with the lady now, sir. Please take your seat and strap in securely. *[calls out to colleague, Hemal]* Hemal – I need some help. Get the first aid kit immediately.

Hemal   OK. *[pause – takes trolley back to galley and talks to another flight attendant]* Jutta, can you secure my trolley for me please, and call Ted to inform him we have a passenger with a head injury in Zone D, and that Leila is dealing with it.

 6.2

Leila   Is she travelling with you, sir?

Man   No, I think she's alone. I haven't spoken to her, but I don't think she's travelling with anyone.

Leila   Hello, hello. How are you feeling?

Woman   Ooh. Everything just went black.

Leila   Do you have any pain?

Woman   I'm a bit dizzy, that's all.

Leila   You've had a nasty bang on your head. How are you feeling?

Woman   Not too bad.

Leila   Would you like a glass of water?

Woman   Yes, that would be good.

Leila   You've got a small cut on your forehead. It doesn't look too serious, though. I'm going to clean up the wound and put a dressing over it.

Leila   Do you feel well enough to sit up?

Woman   I'm fine.

Hemal   Here's the first aid kit. How is she?

Leila   She's feeling all right. Thanks, Hemal. Can you get her a glass of water, please?

Hemal   Yes, I'll get one.

Woman   I'm all right. I was a bit dizzy, but I'm fine now.

Leila   I'm glad you're feeling all right. Can you hold this compress against your forehead? The captain has switched on the seatbelts sign, so if you feel able to sit up, I could help you into your seat. I'll fasten your seatbelt for you and come back and check how you are in a few moments.

 6.3

What's happened?
Are you all right?
Can you hear me?
How are you feeling?
Do you have any pain?
Do you feel well enough to sit up?
How is she?
Can you hold this compress against your forehead?
Can you get her a glass of water, please?

 6.4

Man   Hey, come quickly. There's a man back here. He's unconscious.

Rani   OK, where is he? Bilal, grab the oxygen and a defibrillator from the medical kit and get Safiya to call Anton, to advise him of a medical emergency.

Bilal   OK.

[Short pause]

Safiya   Hello, Anton. This is Safiya here from Economy cabin. We have a medical emergency on board …

Rani   Hello, Can you hear me? *[to his wife:]* Are you travelling with this passenger?

Woman   I'm his wife. Oh my goodness, I think he's had a heart attack. He said he had a bit of indigestion – that was all. He stood up to go to the toilet and then he collapsed.

Rani   He's very grey. He's not breathing. Let's get him on the floor now. … Oh, he's breathing again. *[to wife]* Has this ever happened before?

Woman   No.

Rani   Bilal, help me get the mask over his head. *[to ill man]* Can you hear me?

Rani   *[to other passengers]* Please move away and return to your seats. He needs as much air as possible. Sit down, please. Thank you. Bilal, I think we're going to need a doctor. Can you make an announcement immediately? *[to wife]* Is he on any medication?

Woman   Yes, he's a diabetic so he has injections for that. Is he going to be all right?

Rani   Don't worry. We're taking care of him. How old is he?

Woman   Sixty-three.

Rani   And in good health usually?

Woman   Yes, but he's been very tired recently.

Bilal   Ladies and gentleman – if there is a doctor on board, please make yourself known to a member of the crew immediately by pressing your call bell. Thank you.

Doctor   I'm a doctor, what's the problem?

Woman   Oh, thank goodness.

Rani   Hello doctor, thank you for coming forward. This passenger is unconscious and he stopped breathing for a few seconds. We administered CPR for two minutes and he's breathing again, although his pulse is very weak and his breathing is shallow. We're just administering oxygen …

 6.5

Bilal, grab the oxygen.
Get Safiya to call Anton.
Help me get the mask over his head.
Tell the captain.
Make an announcement immmediately.

6.6

Captain   So what is the situation with the passenger?

Anton   We have a doctor on board who is with the passenger at the moment. However, it's a very serious situation. The doctor has said the passenger is going into cardiac arrest and has requested the aircraft should divert to the nearest hospital urgently.

Captain   Right. You're absolutely certain?

Anton   Yes, Captain.

Captain   Is the passenger travelling with anybody else?

Anton   His wife is with him. She's naturally highly stressed and anxious.

Captain   Right, I need the passenger's details immediately. I'll contact ATC and make the necessary arrangements, and I'll be back in touch with you in a minute.

Anton   OK.

 6.7

Captain   Ladies and gentlemen, this is an important announcement. We have a serious medical situation on board and we need to divert to Mumbai, the nearest airport, as soon as possible. The flight attendants will now prepare the cabin for landing. I anticipate being on the ground within the next 15 minutes. After landing at Mumbai, you must remain on board the aircraft. I do apologize for any inconvenience this diversion may cause, however, I'd like to thank you for your cooperation and understanding. After landing at Mumbai, we will keep you regularly updated with our plans for your continued flight today.

 6.8

Ladies and gentlemen – if there is a doctor on board, please make yourself known to a member of the crew immediately by pressing your call bell. Thank you.

 6.9

/t/: collapsed, checked, stopped, asked, switched

/d/: loosened, happened, resumed, informed, arrived, closed, remained, administered, suffered

/ɪd/: wanted, reported, fainted, needed, decided, assisted, recommended

Unit 7

 7.1

Purser   Ladies and gentlemen, this is an emergency. This is an emergency. Stay in your seats with your seatbelts fastened. Remain calm and follow these instructions. Pull down the oxygen mask. Pull down the oxygen mask. Put it over your nose and mouth immediately and breathe normally.

FA   Grab your mask. Pull it down and place it over your nose and mouth.

Purser   Remain calm. Stay in your seats and pull a mask towards you. Place the mask over your mouth and nose like this and breathe normally, adjusting the band to secure it. Do make sure your own mask is fitted properly before helping anyone else.

 7.2

Stay in your seats.
Remain calm.
Pull down the oxygen mask.
Pull it down over your nose and mouth.
Breathe normally.

 7.3

Captain   Ladies and gentlemen, your captain speaking. We have a technical problem and for everyone's safety we've decided to land in the next 20 minutes at the nearest airport. The landing should be perfectly normal, but for safety reasons we will evacuate the aircraft using the slides. The cabin crew will now give you full instructions and prepare you for the landing. Please listen carefully to their instructions. Thank you.

 7.4

Purser   Ladies and gentlemen. As the captain has just told you, we shall be landing in 20 minutes. For safety reasons, after landing we shall be leaving the aircraft using the evacuation slides. So please listen very carefully and do exactly as instructed. Please return to your seats immediately and keep your seatbelt fastened securely.

We are now going to take you through our safety procedures. Please watch and listen carefully. The safety card in your seat pocket shows details of your escape routes, oxygen masks and lifejackets. It also shows the bracing position, which you must adopt in an emergency landing. Again, please listen carefully.

Emergency exits are on both sides of the aircraft. They are clearly marked and are being pointed out to you now. On the main deck there are two exits at the rear of the First class cabin and two at the front and rear of each other cabin section. On the upper deck there is an emergency exit on each side, in the middle of the cabin.

Please take a moment now to locate the exit nearest to you, bearing in mind that the nearest usable exit may be behind you. To help you find your way to the exits, additional lighting is provided in the aisles at floor level.

Please remain seated and follow instructions given to you by your crew. Do not leave your seats until instructed to do so by your crew. When the seatbelt signs are switched off, make your way to your nearest exit. Leave all personal belongings behind. I repeat, leave all personal hand baggage behind. Ladies, remove high-heeled shoes, as they may tear the slide.

 7.5

The captain told the crew to prepare the cabin for an emergency landing.
The flight attendant told the passengers to take off their shoes.
The flight attendant told the passengers not to get anything from the overhead lockers.
The purser told the passengers not to worry.

UNIT 8

 8.1

1

Man Excuse me, we've been waiting for drinks for a long time. We finished eating twenty minutes ago.

FA Oh, I do understand. I apologize. It's been so busy. What can I get you?

2

Woman I'm sorry, I can't eat this meal – it's cold!

FA Oh dear, that's not good. I'm really sorry. Let me take it away for you and see if I can get you a hot cooked meal immediately.

3

Woman This is not what I asked for. I ordered a vegetarian meal!

FA Oh, dear. I'm sorry about this. Please be patient. Let me just check the special meals list.

8.2

Let me just check the special meals list.
Let me get an official form for you.
Let me see if I can get you another one.
Let me get you a blanket.

8.3

1

The toilets are dirty and the smell is disgusting.

2

We've asked for the cabin to be made a little warmer and it's getting even colder.

3

Excuse me, why doesn't someone tell us why there is such a long delay?

4

Listen, it's not good enough. First we were given the wrong seats and now we are surrounded by crying babies.

5

I want to make an official complaint. There were no snacks, the plane hadn't been cleaned and the service was awful.

8.4

1

Woman The toilets are dirty and the smell is disgusting.

FA Thank you for letting me know and I do apologize. I'll make sure they are dealt with immediately. As soon as they have been cleaned, I'll come back to let you know.

2

Man We've asked for the cabin to be made a little warmer and it's getting even colder.

FA Yes, I'm sorry about this. We seem to have a slight technical problem with the cabin temperature at the moment but we are sorting it out. It should warm up in about five minutes. Let me get you a blanket in the meantime.

3

Man Excuse me, why doesn't someone tell us why there is such a long delay?

FA I do apologize, sir. I know how frustrating it is sitting here and not knowing what's going on. Unfortunately, the jetty got stuck and so we couldn't close the door. However, we expect to be pushing back in five minutes.

4

Man Listen, it's not good enough. First we were given the wrong seats and now we are surrounded by crying babies.

FA I'm sorry about that. You're right. I have a couple of empty seats in a quieter part of the cabin a little further down. You'd be welcome to move to those.

5

Woman I want to make an official complaint. There were no snacks, the plane hadn't been cleaned and the service was awful.

FA I'm sorry that you haven't enjoyed your flight. We've had so many problems today and I can only apologize. I'll get an official complaint form for you this very minute.

8.5

Man Excuse me, listen, I can't sit here any longer. That group of people is making too much noise. They are disturbing me and everyone around. If you can't do anything about it, you'll have to find me another seat. I refuse to sit here any longer.

Josef Hmm, yes, I understand. I can hear how noisy they are, and I'm sorry they are disturbing you. Have you spoken to them yourself?

Man Of course not. I don't think they care about me or anyone else.

Josef Let me have a word with them. If it doesn't get better, then I'll try to find you another seat, although the plane is pretty full. How about that?

Man Well, er … yes, OK. Thank you. That would be fine.

8.6

Josef Hans, I need your help.

Hans What's the problem, Josef?

Josef Can you see that guy standing in the middle with his arms folded?

Hans Yes. He looks upset and angry.

Josef He is. He wants me to tell the group behind him to keep quiet or else he is demanding a seat change. I wondered if there were any seats vacant in the next cabin in case I have to re-seat him?

Hans Out of the question. The plane's full. There aren't any spare seats anywhere.

Josef OK. I'll go over and tell the group to quieten down.

Hans I think that's the best thing.

Josef I just hope they'll be reasonable!

Hans You'll be fine! Just use your usual charm and ask them to be a little quieter!

Josef Hans, if you see me struggling, please could you come over to help me?

Hans You'll be fine, don't worry. I'll keep an eye on you. If there is still a problem, then I'll come over.

8.7

Josef Excuse me, excuse me. Listen guys, are you enjoying the flight?

Man 1 Yes, yes, sure.

Man 2 You bet, it's great.

Josef Great. Could I ask you a special favour? Would you mind just keeping your voices down a little? You're getting a little loud and some people are trying to sleep or watch a film.

Man 1 Why? Who's complaining?

Man 2 Are we making a lot of noise?

Josef No-one's complained, but we can hear you all in the galley!

Man 1 Oh, OK, no problem.

Man 2 OK.

Man 1 How about another drink?

Josef Sure, I'll get you another drink if you keep your voices down. Thanks for your understanding.

8.8

If the situation doesn't get better, then I'll try to find you another seat.

If there's still a problem, then I'll come over.

If there is still a problem, I won't leave you on your own.

I'll get you another drink if you keep your voices down.

8.9

Could I ask you a special favour?

Would you mind just keeping the noise down a little?

Please could you come over to help me?

8.10

Man Hey you, where's my vodka? I've been waiting ages for it.

Jenny I'm sorry sir. The bar is now closed. We're not serving drinks.

Man Why not?

Jenny I've already said sir, the drinks service has finished, sir. The bar is closed.

Man I asked before. I ... I want another vodka. Get me another vodka, I said. Hey, come here. Get me a vodka!

Jenny Just one moment, sir.

Man I demand that you get me a drink! I asked you for a drink and you said you were going to get one. That was 15 minutes ago. So I want my drink! Do you hear me!

Jenny *[On the intercom]* Hello Tom, we've got a guy in 36D who's had too much to drink and he wants more. He's becoming very aggressive verbally and physically. I think we're going to need the restraining straps. Call Ted immediately.

Tom Just tell him, no more, finished, that's it.

Jenny I did, and he started shouting and then he pushed me. Almost knocked me over. We have a problem. Tell Ted, please.

Tom OK. Will do. And I'm on my way.

Jenny Sir, we can't serve any more drinks. Please sit down, sir.

Man Well if you won't get me one, I'll go and get it myself!

Tom I'm afraid the bar is closed sir. Please sit down. You have to sit down, sir. Sit down, I said. I'm warning you, sir.

Tom Ted, give us a hand to control him.

Ted Get him to the seat just there. That's it. I'll strap his wrist to the armrest. Good, now the other. That will hold him in his seat.

Tom He's shouting and swearing – he's not calming down at all.

Ted Yes, the situation is becoming serious now. I have to speak to the captain. I think we're going to need to have the police meet the aircraft on arrival.

Tom Right.

Ted Tom, stay with him. Reassure the passengers the situation is being dealt with. I'll be back in a moment.

Tom Right.

8.11

You have to sit down, sir.

I have to speak to the captain.

You have to stop that now.

You have to be quiet.

You have to do what the captain says.

8.12

Would you come to the back of the plane with me, please, madam?

I can see how upset you are.

Can you tell me exactly what happened?

I do apologize. Incidents like this are extremely rare.

Please don't worry.

Everything is under control.

UNIT 9

9.1

Purser Ladies and gentlemen, we'll shortly be landing at Montreal Trudeau Airport. The 'Fasten seatbelts' signs have been switched on. Please return to your seat and ensure your hand-baggage is safely secured in the overhead lockers or under the seat in front of you. Please also make sure your table is folded away, your seat back is upright, with the arm-rest down and your seatbelt is fastened.

Passengers seated in our First and Business class cabins, please make sure that your foot-rest and video screens are back in their original position.

If you have been using the in-seat power, we will shortly be switching it off, so please now unplug your laptop and store it in a safe place.

Once again, may we remind you that cell phones must not be switched on until the seatbelt signs have been switched off after landing.

We hope that you've enjoyed the in-flight entertainment during the flight. In preparation for landing we'll be switching the system off. It would greatly assist the flight attendants if you could have your used headsets ready for collection as they pass through the cabin.

9.2

1

Please return to your seat and ensure your hand-baggage is safely secured in the overhead lockers or under the seat in front of you.

2

Please make sure that your foot rest and video screens are back in their original position.

3

If you have been using the in-seat power, we will shortly be switching it off, so please now unplug your laptop and store it in a safe place.

4

May we remind you that cell phones must not be switched on until the seatbelt signs have been switched off after landing.

 9.3

FA Thank you so much. Can you open the window blind, please? Brilliant ... and put your tray table away. Thanks.

Woman Excuse me, I can't find my arrival form – you know the customs thing.

FA You mean, the disembarkation form?

Woman That's it.

FA No problem, I'll bring you one in a few minutes.

Woman Thanks a lot. Do you want my headphones?

FA Not me, my colleague will collect them soon. ... Hello there. Put your bags under the seats in front, please. Perfect. ... Ah, this is an exit row, so everything has to go in the overhead lockers, please. Nothing on the floor at all. OK? Thanks for that.

Man 1 Can I give you these magazines?

FA Sure. Anything else? No? OK.

Man 2 Sorry to bother you. Do you know how long it takes to get from the airport to the city?

FA Yes, I do. By bus, by train, or by taxi?

Man 2 Which is the best?

FA To be honest, I'm not sure – we take the company minibus and it takes about half an hour to the city centre.

Man 2 That's not bad.

FA Everyone says the train is the fastest, but double check.

Man 2 Fantastic. Many thanks for your help.

FA Enjoy your stay there. ... Your seat back please, sir. Thank you, and your tray table. Good. And, sorry, could you take your coat off the empty seat and put it in the locker, please?

 9.4

Man Excuse me.

FA Yes, how can I help?

Man The captain said we were landing 15 minutes ago, but we seem to be climbing again.

FA Yes, you're right.

Man What's wrong? Does this mean a delay?

FA I'm not sure. There might be a short delay. This airport can be very busy first thing in the morning. If there is a delay, the captain will make an announcement.

Man Oh, dear.

FA Is there a problem?

Man I have to make a quick connection to Nice.

FA I see. Well, let's see if we can get you off the plane first if there is a delay.

Man Thank you.

9.5

First officer Ladies and gentlemen, This is the first officer speaking. Unfortunately I have some bad news for you. Air Traffic Control has advised us that, due to a problem on the ground, we will be delayed for approximately 30 minutes or so. My apologies for any inconvenience, but we'll get you on the ground as quickly as possible. In the meantime, please keep your seatbelts fastened.

Man So there is a delay after all. Do we know why?

FA I'm afraid I can't tell you any more than what the first officer said.

Man Listen, I'm in transit. I've got a connecting flight and not a lot of time.

FA I know. You told me. What time is your flight to Nice?

Man At 10.15.

FA OK. Well, if we land at nine you should be OK.

Man How long does it take to get to the domestic terminal? I've only got hand luggage and I'm checked through, but I do have to clear immigration in Paris, don't I?

FA Yes, I'm afraid so. It takes about five minutes to get to the terminal you need. Look, all I can say is we'll get you off the plane as fast as possible.

Man Fingers crossed.

 9.6

Leila Tom, sorry, have you checked your side of the cabin?

Tom Yes.

Leila Good. Could you check Jutta's side for me, then? She still hasn't finished the bar paperwork, for Customs.

Tom Oh, right. No problem.

Leila Also, she says you took the bar seals out of the bar trolley. Where did you put them?

Tom Oh, I think they're in the galley.

Leila If you could give them to her, that would be great. By the way, is your side of the cabin secure yet?

Tom Not quite. I've still got a bit of clearing in to do and I've got to put one bassinet away.

Leila OK.

Tom Oh, and one passenger is still in the toilet.

Leila Right. You'd better bang on the door and get him to his seat fast.

Tom OK.

Leila Do that first and clear in the cabin on the way back.

Tom Sure. But does Jutta need any help with the C209s?

Leila Don't worry, I'll help Jutta. You haven't got time.

Tom OK.

Leila Let me know when your cabin is secure so I can give the checks to Hemal.

Jutta OK. I've done the customs paperwork.

Leila Are all the bars locked and sealed?

Jutta Yes.

Leila OK, go and help Tom. He's checking your side of the cabin – you could take a tray and clear in any rubbish in the cabin. But you'll have to be quick.

Tom OK, Leila, cabin and galley now secure.

First officer *[on intercom]* Cabin crew seats for landing.

Leila Well done! Just in time. Better grab our seats and strap in quickly. *[on intercom]* Hemal, cabin secure.

Hemal Great. Thanks! See you after landing!

 9.7

Has she done the final checks? No, she hasn't.

Have you secured the trolley in the galley? Yes, I have.

Have they checked the tables are upright? No, they haven't.

Have we done everything? Yes, we have.

Unit 10

 10.1

Purser Ladies and gentlemen, on behalf of the captain and the entire crew we would like to welcome you to Boston, where the local time is 14.55.

For your safety, please remain seated with your seatbelt fastened, leaving all items of hand-luggage safely stowed, until the seatbelt signs have been switched off.

Before you leave the aircraft, please ensure that you have all your personal items and hand-luggage with you. Please be careful when opening overhead lockers as items may fall out causing injury.

We would like to remind you that smoking is not permitted until you've reached a designated smoking area outside the terminal building. We would also like to remind all passengers that mobile phones should not be switched on until the seatbelt signs have been turned off.

As the captain told you, it is very cold outside so I suggest you have your coats ready for when you get outside the terminal!

We wish you a very pleasant stay or a safe journey if you are continuing your journey. We hope to see you again in the future. Goodbye.

 10.2

the entire crew
the local time
safely stowed
please ensure
please be careful
designated area
terminal building

 10.3

Captain OK, everyone. This debriefing will be short, as I'm sure we're all very tired. As you know, our flight was quite turbulent, but judging by the positive comments from our passengers, you all worked extremely hard to ensure passenger safety at all times. It was also good hearing passengers saying how much they'd enjoyed their flight in the circumstances as they left the aircraft. So I'd like to thank you all for a job well done. Ted?

Ted Thanks, Captain. Yes, in general, it was a good flight. However, our flight had two incidents, and we should talk about them now. In both cases, our teamwork was not the best. The first incident involved shutting down the meals service due to turbulence. The 'Fasten seatbelts' sign came on which means ...

Mixed voices ... shut down ... end of service ... everyone sitting down.

Ted That's right. So what happened, Leila?

Leila Yes, sorry, Ted. I heard the 'passengers and crew to their seats' announcement clearly and I just assumed my crew would immediately help to secure the cabin and galley. However, I should've checked on my crew. Hemal and Jutta were dealing with a difficult passenger, not realizing a sense of urgency.

Ted You should've told them to stop.

Leila You're right. I should have communicated better with my crew.

Ted OK. And what about the coffee pots spillage?

Leila Again, we should act more promptly in future as a team to secure the cabin or galley. During the turbulence, one trolley was still in the cabin and overturned. All the coffee pots fell on the floor.

Ted OK. What can you do next time should a similar situation occur?

Leila As soon as I hear the announcement, I won't make assumptions! I will immediately communicate with my crew to ensure they've heard the announcement and understood the instructions. I will then make sure that all in-flight service is halted until further notice is given by you or the captain. I will also make sure that the cabin and galley is secured as quickly as possible.

Ted Right. It's vital to check your crew have understood any communication via the PA system – so a valuable lesson learned today. Has anyone else got anything they'd like to say about the flight? OK, then ...

 10.4

We should talk about two incidents now.
You should act more promptly in future.
You shouldn't continue serving food next time.
You should've shut down the service immediately.
You should've told them to stop
I should've communicated better.
We shouldn't have been late.

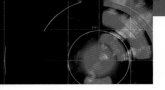

Answer key

Unit 1

Meeting colleagues

1 1 Boston
2 'My name's Paola, by the way.'
3 'Hi, Paola. I'm Tom. It's nice to meet you.'
4 'Sorry, what's your name?'
5 They are not sure. Possibly.
6 in ten minutes' time

2 1 F (They greet each other by name.)
2 F – 'We've met before.'
3 T
4 F (She wants to do some shopping there.)
5 T
6 F (It was Jenny who spilled the drinks.)
7 F (Katrin isn't.)

3 1 Ted
2 in Business
3 in Economy
4 It's her first long-haul flight.
5 Leila and Hemal
6 at Door 4 Left

Finding out about the flight

1 Possible order: 4, 2, 3, 5, 6, 1
2 1 his first officer, Rick Schultz
2 that they have a quick flight time to Boston
3 the weather during the flight
4 turbulence expected after 3½ hours
5 the main cabin service
6 finish the meals and drinks service early
7 that the crew know the cockpit procedures

3 1 moderate   4 strapped
2 strong   5 cockpit
3 over

Case study

1 1 the emergency equipment, the safety instruction card, the number of meals on board, the usual drinks trolley and duty-free goods, and that the toilets are all stocked with the necessary hand towels and tissues
2 security and the aircraft's safety features

5 1 partly terrified, very excited
2 The actual content was always the same; the atmosphere could be different – sometimes friendly, sometimes tense.
3 VIPs / celebrities; passengers who are travelling for sad reasons

Unit 2

Welcoming passengers

3 three (although the second woman is travelling with someone else)
4 1 Good   2 Can   3 how   4 May
5 The passenger asked for a window seat, but has not got one.
6 1 False. There are some empty seats.
2 17D
3 because she doesn't want an aisle seat
4 at check-in
5 She will move her as soon as she has checked the passenger list.
6 She asks the passenger to remain in the aisle seat until she has checked the passenger list.

7 1 airline   5 first name
2 boarding time   6 date
3 flight number   7 seat number
4 family name   8 gate number
8 1 check-in   6 window seats
2 hand-baggage   7 in advance
3 boarding pass   8 hand-baggage
4 seat number   9 overhead lockers
5 Seating arrangements

Settling passengers in their seats

1 1 head-rest   6 table
2 seatbelt   7 safety
3 arm-rest   instruction card
4 overhead locker 8 call button
5 TV handset   9 light button
   control
2 1 the passenger list
2 move the passenger to 15A
3 help her with her bags
4 her first name
3 She has an 11-month-old baby with her.
4 1 after take-off
2 'How old is your baby?'; 'Has she flown before?'

3 a bit nervous, especially about the baby waking up during take-off
4 on her mother's lap
5 with a special baby belt
6 1 T
2 F (He says he was delayed getting to the airport from the city.)
3 F (Sylvie says 'No problem.')
4 T
5 F (Sylvie says 'Everyone is on board.')
7 1 see   5 expecting
2 sorry   6 cross
3 getting   7 that's it
4 airport   8 secure

Demonstrating safety procedures and checking before take-off

1 A 1 B 4 C 8 D 5 E 9 F 6 G 11 H 12
   I 10 J 2 K 7 L 3 M 13
5 a 5 b 1 c 2 d 6 e 3 f 4 g 7 h 8

Case study

1 1 the growing problems of storing hand-baggage in the overhead lockers as passengers board the aircraft
2 Yes. If there is no space for their bags in the overhead lockers or under the seat in front of them, their bags will be off-loaded and put in the hold.
2 1 People become angry; flight attendants are stressed because they can't perform their proper duties.
2 store small items under seats, leave space for others, free the aisles
3 safety duties: checking equipment and passengers' behaviour / needs
5 1 The business traveller who is serious; passengers going on holiday, maybe flying for the first time, who are excited and nervous; passengers travelling to visit family and friends. All have different feelings.
2 He was an elderly man with an obviously serious medical condition. Shon had to decide whether to allow him to travel or not. He wanted to travel. He was taken off the plane by paramedics, and a possibly serious medical incident was avoided.

3 to do the job with the most professional and highest standard possible

Her tips: drink plenty of water, carry a little pot of moisturiser for the lips. For women, take a new bottle of nail varnish; for men, moisturiser

Unit 3

Making the first announcements

2 1 board   6 block
   2 unless   7 ready
   3 quickly   8 through
   4 Sorry   9 orders
   5 free   10 exact

3 1 2 and 3
   2 1 (There are no hot snacks.)
   3 3

5 1 It's **great** to have you on board.
   2 **Please** don't leave your **seats** unless you **have** to.
   3 We'd like to serve you **drinks** and **snacks** as **quickly** as possible.
   4 The **seatbelt** sign is **off**.
   5 Feel **free** to walk **around**.
   6 **Thanks** for your cooperation.
   7 We shall be coming through the cabin with **refreshments** in a few **moments**.
   8 We'd **really** appreciate it if you had the **exact change** for your purchases.

Getting started

2 1 go to the toilet
   2 a glass of water
   3 heat her baby's bottle
   4 how long it takes to get from Terminal 2 to Terminal 3

3 1 sit   4 help   7 do
   2 problem   5 with   8 worry
   3 course   6 soon   9 get

Helping to settle passengers

2 Passenger 1: She can't get her bag down from the overhead locker.
Passenger 2: He needs a blanket.
Passenger 3: He wants his meal.
Passenger 4: She wants to change seats.

3 Passenger 1: Are you feeling better now?
Passenger 2: Can I help you, sir?
Passenger 3: Did you call, sir?
Passenger 4: Is everything all right?

5 1 how long the flight will be
   2 11 hours
   3 at 10.45 / in 45 minutes' time
   4 They are hungry.
   5 headphones for her girls/children
   6 channel 2
   7 a blanket
   8 to remind herself about the blanket

Case study

1 1 children kicking the backs of seats; families talking loudly and passing things backwards and forwards; babies crying loudly
   2 Some passengers want parents to control children more, some suggest 'family-only' zones on board. Cabin crew can ask parents to control children. Airlines sometimes provide cards/colouring books on the aircraft, and tables/chairs/toys at the departure gate.

4 1 getting the drinks trolleys ready for the first service; dealing with passengers' queries
   2 The biggest difference is the need for speed on short-haul flights. Shon preferred long-haul because of the exotic destinations and, above all, the chance to interact with passengers.
   3 During take-off an elderly man held on to her foot without realizing it.

Unit 4

Giving a choice

1 1 breakfast and lunch
   2 three   3 three
   4 probably in the morning, as breakfast is served first

2 Fruit: orange, strawberries
Meat/Fish: seafood, chicken, beef tenderloin
Vegetables/Herbs: seasonal salad, tomatoes, cauliflower, onions, beans, peas, chives, potatoes, red pepper, green salad
Dairy food: yoghurt, butter, Parmesan (cheese), cheese sauce, cream

3 1 dessert   5 knife   9 butter
   2 first course   6 roll   10 napkin / / salad   7 main   serviette
   3 cup   course
   4 fork   8 spoon

4 1 T
   2 F (He chooses red wine.)
   3 F (It is South African.)
   4 True, but this is not on the menu.
   5 T (She asks 'Is the chicken very spicy?' and she says 'Good.' when told it is 'just mildly spiced'.)
   6 F (She asks for a special children's meal.)
   7 T (She hasn't pre-ordered a children's menu.)
   8 F (She chooses still water for herself and 7up for her children.)
   9 T

Serving drinks

2 | Wines and beers | Spirits |
| --- | --- |
| Sauvignon Blanc | Johnny Walker |
| Merlot | cognac |
| Bloody Mary | vodka |
| Martini | Bacardi rum |
| Kronenberg | bourbon |
| port | **Soft drinks** |
| Carlsberg | soda |
| Bordeaux | Perrier |
| champagne | apple juice |
| **Hot drinks** | diet Coke |
| fruit tea | lemonade |
| hot chocolate | bottled still water |
| cappuccino | tomato juice |
| Earl Grey tea | tonic water |
| English Breakfast tea | ginger ale |
| espresso | |

3 a 7   b 4   c 3   d 1   e 6   f 2
   g 9   h 5   i 8

4 1 No, she doesn't.
   2 four
   3 He wants tea, but will have to wait because only cold drinks are being served.
   4 two
   5 'Here we are. Enjoy.'
   6 Yes, he says the meal is great.
   7 because the bar is shut
   8 a soft drink

Duty-free sales

1 1 begin   2 list   3 pocket   4 using
   5 accept   6 win   7 excellent

2 1 shortly   4 frequent flyers
   2 purchases   5 bargains
   3 prepare   6 designed

3

Perfumes & jewellery	Electric & electronic items
a brooch	a USB key
perfume spray	a travel plug adaptor
earrings	a travel razor
eau de toilette	headphones
a crystal pendant	
a bracelet	

Alcohol & tobacco	Cosmetics	Gifts
whisky	face cream	a soft toy
cognac	aftershave	chocolates
cigars	lipstick	a watch
vodka	mascara	a model aircraft
champagne		a scarf
cigarettes		a pen

4 1 perfume
  2 $41
  3 a scarf
  4 by credit card
  5 because he wants his frequent flyer points
  6 a receipt

6 1 $46.50
  2 $8.25
  3 €56.75
  4 €13.50
  5 £22.90
  6 $40.59

7 Spain/euro, China/renminbi, Brazil/real, Australia/Australian dollar, UAE/dirham, Singapore/Singapore dollar, Saudi Arabia/Saudi riyal, Russia/rouble, Nigeria/naira, Pakistan/rupee

Case study

1 1 Passengers = 1, 2, 3, 8, 9, 10
    Crew = 4,5,6   Either = 7
  2 positive: 1, 3 and 10; negative: 2, 3, 7, 8 and 9 (3 contains both negative and positive comments); no opinion: 4, 5 and 6
  3 positive: fine, well prepared, look great, taste even better
    negative: the worst, bland, not very hot, badly presented, tasteless, dreadful, not fit for human consumption

4 1 because she had the chance to engage with the passengers and get to know them
  2 during the pre-flight briefing; the number of meals and the nature of any special meals needed
  3 The woman's children were given food from First and Business class.

Unit 5

Identifying passenger problems

2 1 get the sound to work on his headphones
  2 no
  3 Yes. He alters the volume.
  4 A film (movie) – *The English Patient*
  5 Yes. He selects the film for her.

4 1 i   2 e   3 d   4 a

5 1 information officer   3 nanny
  2 waiter(ress)   4 nurse

Dealing with problems

2 1 He offers to check on their arrival time.
  2 a sandwich
  3 a blanket
  4 no
  5 She offers to try to find a doctor or nurse.

3 1 get back   4 see
  2 get   5 ask
  3 meantime

Saying sorry

2 peppermint tea, tomato juice, cheese sandwiches

3 1 Passenger 3: 'I don't believe it – it's the same old story.
    You always seem to run out.'
  2 Passenger 3: 'They've been very popular today.'
  3 four
  4 Seven, if you include 'I'm afraid we've only got apple juice and orange juice today'.

4 1 get   5 chicken   9 way
  2 sandwiches   6 same   10 about
  3 run   7 seem
  4 popular   8 apologize

Case study

1 1 Thousands of pounds in cash was stolen from passengers as they slept on the overnight flight from Tokyo to Paris.
  2 at least six passengers, in Business class
  3 No. The airline did not comment on this particular incident, but said that in general passengers' belongings in the cabin are their own responsibility.

4 1 Usually most airlines provide a week or possibly two weeks of customer service training and one week, or half, of that training is centred on handling passenger complaints.
  2 the seating and the choice of meals
  3 show that you understand the passenger's point of view, and deal with their problem

Unit 6

Dealing with an on-board accident

2 1 a female passenger in row 20
  2 a head wound
  3 During the turbulence a laptop fell out of the overhead locker onto her head.
  4 to take his seat and strap in securely
  5 to get the first aid kit immediately

3 1 No one. She is alone.
  2 a bit dizzy
  3 a glass of water
  4 a small cut
  5 clean up the wound and put a dressing over it
  6 hold a compress against her forehead; get into her seat and strap in

4 1 hurt; bleeding   5 dressing
  2 fell   6 dizzy
  3 feeling   7 hold
  4 bang

6 1 automatic external defibrillator (AED)
  2 cardiopulmonary resuscitation (CPR) mask
  3 aspirin   7 syringes
  4 antiseptic wipes   8 oxygen
  5 gloves   9 stethoscope
  6 bandages   10 dressings

Dealing with a serious medical incident

2 1 T
  2 F (He is travelling with his wife.)
  3 F (She wants to put him on the floor.)
  4 F
  5 T
  6 F (They need a doctor.)
  7 T (He is a diabetic and has injections.)
  8 F (He is 63. He's been tired recently.)
  9 T
  10 F

3 1 hear   5 mask
   2 heart   6 care
   3 breathing   7 administered
   4 get   8 pulse

6 1 that the man is going into cardiac arrest
   2 yes
   3 that they divert the plane to the nearest hospital without delay
   4 The captain will contact ATC and arrange to land at the nearest airport.

7 1 important   5 anticipate
   2 divert   6 remain
   3 nearest   7 inconvenience
   4 prepare   8 updated

Reporting a medical incident

2 /t/: checked, stopped, asked, switched
/d/: happened, resumed, informed, arrived, closed, remained, administered, suffered
/ɪd/: reported, fainted, needed, decided, assisted, recommended

5 1 happened   8 administer
   2 cardiac   9 recommended
   3 condition   10 aware
   4 comfortable   11 services
   5 pulse   12 until
   6 defibrillator   13 transferred
   7 first   14 resumed

Case study

1 1 A doctor responded to the call from cabin crew and ended up treating several patients.
   2 three – none of them serious medical emergencies
   3 fetching equipment the doctor needed; administering oxygen

4 1 1 fractures   4 strokes
     2 hyperventilation   5 giving birth
     3 heart attacks   6 nose bleed
   3 Two main reasons: first, flight attendants' medical training is excellent and they are taught how to deal with a wide range of situations that can occur on board; second, there is always someone on board (doctor/nurse or experienced crew member) who will know how to deal with medical problems.

Unit 7

Taking charge in an emergency

4 1 emergency   9 over
   2 emergency   10 mouth
   3 Stay   11 normally
   4 fastened   12 over
   5 calm   13 mouth
   6 follow   14 pull
   7 down   15 band
   8 down   16 before

Preparing for an emergency evacuation

2 1 speaking   5 slides
   2 technical   6 prepare
   3 20 (twenty)   7 carefully
   4 normal

4 1 leaving   9 marked
   2 evacuation   10 pointed
   3 exactly   11 locate
   4 keep   12 additional
   5 going   13 belongings
   6 shows   14 behind
   7 bracing   15 remove
   8 sides

Reporting an evacuation

1 an aircraft floating on water; people standing or sitting on the wings and on the evacuation slides

4 1 a bird-strike   3 none
   2 on water in the   4 the captain
      Hudson River   5 good training

5 1 massive   6 slightly
   2 a strike   7 submerged
   3 to survive   8 injuries
   4 to ditch   9 first-class
   5 floating   10 superbly

Case study

1 1 a 3   b 1   c 7   d 5   e 8   f 6   g 2   h 4
   2 The cabin crew moved passengers to other seats and even tried to release oxygen mask with their ID cards.

4 1 V1: There was instrument failure just before V1, which is the point at which an aircraft is committed to leaving the ground.
braking: This caused the aircraft to swerve violently.
senior crew member: He was so scared Shon could see the veins in his neck.

people in the Business class section: She could see the fear in their faces, and the knuckles on their hands were white as they held on tightly to their arm-rests.
communication from the flight deck: There wasn't any (presumably the crew were too busy trying to control the aircraft).

   2 the announcements from the captain: The captain's communication skills were excellent.
the tyres on the aircraft: All the tyres except three had burst.
the fuel tanks: They were in the wings, so the captain didn't want the exit doors over the wings to be opened, although two passengers did open them; fortunately they did not explode.
passengers behaving selfishly: One woman with two children jumped out before them, leaving them at the top of the evacuation slide; one man was determined to take his briefcase, blocking the escape of other passengers; two passengers opened the wing doors, despite instructions not to.

3 1 cope   2 stress   3 competent
   4 calm   5 drills   6 approach

Unit 8

Responding to passenger complaints

4 1 apologize; busy; get
   2 good; really; away
   3 dear; patient; special

5 2 Sympathize: Oh dear, that's not good.
Apologize: I'm really sorry.
Find a solution: Let me take it away for you and see if I can get you a hot cooked meal immediately.

3 Sympathize: Oh dear.
Apologize: I'm sorry about this.
Find a solution: Let me just check the special meals list.

7 1 dirty toilets
   2 cold cabin
   3 long delay and no information
   4 wrong seats with crying babies nearby
   5 no snacks, dirty plane, awful service

9 1 letting; apologize 4 sorry; enjoyed
2 frustrating 5 so; only
3 about

Dealing with complaints about other passengers

2 1 A group of people near him are making too much noise.
2 He wants to move.
3 He suggests speaking to the group first and, if that does not work, finding another seat for the passenger.
4 yes, for the moment

3 1 disturbing 4 care
2 refuse 5 word
3 understand 6 How

4 1 No, the plane is full.
2 talk to the noisy passengers
3 just watch the situation and come and help him if necessary

5 1 enjoying 6 noise
2 Great 7 hear
3 favour 8 another
4 down 9 understanding
5 trying

Managing disruptive passengers

2 1 He's drunk and shouting.
2 another drink/vodka
3 very aggressive, verbally and physically
4 get his own drink
5 They restrain him by strapping his wrist to the arm-rest.
6 speak to the captain
7 to have the police meet the aircraft
8 reassure them that the situation is under control

3 1 landing 6 control
2 aggressive 7 strapped
3 alcohol 8 purser
4 shout 9 calm
5 several 10 police

Case study

1 1 interfering with external doors on the aircraft during flight (5)
physically attacking the cabin crew (4)
being abusive to cabin crew (3)
drunken and unruly passengers fighting and disturbing other passengers (2)

passenger becoming abusive before take-off (1)
2 The main cause seems to be too much alcohol. Other causes could be psychologically unbalanced passengers, personal stress, over-assertive behaviour.

4 1 Difficult passengers are frustrating because some problems can't be solved on board in spite of the goodwill and desire of the cabin crew to do their best for them. Shon always worked with the passenger, tried to do the best for them and send them away feeling positive.
2 He complained about everything – the seat, the menu, the towels, the wine, the meal, the blanket, even the bad breath of the flight attendant. But Shon took a positive attitude, never disagreed with him and got him extras and lots of small gifts for his wife. She was extremely kind to him, so much so that when he left the plane, he thanked her and said that although he would never fly with the airline again, his attitude towards its flight attendant (Shon) had changed because she had been so professional.
3 He said he wanted to move because he was very tall and needed more leg-room and he was close to crying babies. Business class was full, so Shon found him a row of seats where he could stretch out. But he wasn't happy because what he had really wanted was an upgrade.

Unit 9

Making final announcements and checks

3 switch off in-seat power, switch off in-flight entertainment system, collect headphones

4 1 shortly 5 away 9 must
2 switched 6 down 10 assist
3 ensure 7 position 11 ready
4 under 8 power

7 1 blind 6 bother
2 arrival 7 takes
3 one 8 minibus
4 front 9 Everyone
5 exit; everything 10 coat; locker

Giving information about delayed landings

2 1 The plane is climbing, not descending.
2 missing a connection to Nice
3 The airport might be busy.
4 getting the passenger off the plane first

3 1 about 30 minutes
2 a problem on the ground
3 nine o'clock
4 10.15
5 clear immigration
6 wait for luggage or check in for his flight to Nice

4 A runway is closed. They divert to Bordeaux.

Getting through the final ten minutes

1 For cabin crew: final checks on passengers; secure everything
For passengers: ten minutes to landing; seatbelts fastened
Next: cabin crew wait for the final warning to take their seats

2 1 yes
2 check Jutta's side
3 She hasn't finished the bar paperwork.
4 He still has some clearing in to do and a bassinet to put away. And there is a passenger in the toilet.
5 get him to his seat
6 yes

3 1 for 3 with 5 on
2 in 4 for 6 to

5 Last 20 minutes: 1, 4, 5, 7, 10, 11
Last 10 minutes: 2, 3, 6, 8, 9, 12

Case study

1 1 All of the ten toilets on board became blocked soon after take-off.
2 The plane had make an unscheduled landing in Mumbai.

4 1 to be collected: meal trays, drinks, headsets, blankets (rubbish also has to be collected, or 'cleared in'); to be checked: landing cards, seatbelts; to be handed out: immigration forms (then also to be checked); to be secured: the cabin, the galley; to be stowed: trolleys

2 She hadn't been given a landing card and there was only ten minutes before landing. Shon's crew had not advised her of this; there was a breakdown in communication. The woman should have been given the forms well in advance of landing.

3 pilot/co-pilot and passengers: minimal communication, usually about the time of arrival, the weather, any delays, thanking passengers for travelling with the airline
passengers and cabin crew: a lot of communication about preparing the passengers for landing (having headsets ready for collection, filling out landing cards and immigration forms, arrival procedures, returning to seats and fastening seatbelts, etc.)
Flight crew and cabin crew: minimal communication apart from advising that passengers and galley are ready for landing and the cabin is secure

Unit 10

Arriving at the gate and disembarking the passengers

3 1 behalf   7 injury
   2 entire   8 designated
   3 items   9 remind
   4 stowed   10 ready
   5 ensure   11 wish
   6 personal

Taking part in the crew debriefing

1 1 a (long haul) / c (short haul)
   2 b   3 c   4 c
2 1 because they are all tired
   2 from positive comments from the passengers
   3 delay in shutting down the meals service and the coffee pots spillage
   4 because they were delayed by a difficult passenger
   5 shut down / end of service / everyone should be sitting down
   6 communicated better with her team
   7 It overturned and all the coffee pots fell on the floor.
   8 a T   b T   c F   d F   e T
5 1 c   2 e   3 a   4 f   5 b   6 d

Case study

1 1 There was a terrorism incident. A man tried to explode a device during the final minutes of normal descent.
   2 The explosive device was a six-inch packet of high explosives called PETN, along with a syringe. It was hidden in the man's underpants.
   3 They reacted quickly. Once they understood what was happening, they jumped on the terrorist, used blankets and a fire extinguisher to put out the flames, restrained the man and put him securely in the front of the plane.
4 1 the cabin, their safety areas, every toilet, every seat and under the seat, the galley areas
   2 those passengers who may be disabled or may have special requirements or special needs
   3 From: hard work, worthwhile, highly rewarding, fun, exciting

Self Study 1

1 1 Hello   5 know
   2 how   6 met
   3 about   7 Pleased
   4 bad   8 meet
2 1 captain   4 purser
   2 flight attendants 5 first officer
   3 cabin supervisor   6 galley leader
3 1 d   2 f   3 e   4 b   5 c   6 a
4 1 credit cards   5 passport
   2 book   6 keys
   3 magazines   7 toothbrush
   4 make-up bag   8 mobile phone
5 1 turbulence   3 storms
   2 winds   4 weather
6 Suggested answers:
   1 b What are cockpit procedures?
         They're flight deck rules and routines.
   2 d What does strapped in mean?
         It means wearing seatbelts.
   3 h What's a roster?
         It's a list of names and duties.
   4 c What's a shuttle?
         It's a crew bus to the aircraft.
   5 a What does long-haul mean?
         It means a long flight.
   6 g What's a log book?
         It's where we write things down.

   7 f What's a passport?
         It's a personal identity document.
   8 e What are stowage areas?
         They're where we put things away.

Self Study 2

1 1 boarding   6 seats
   2 exit   7 change
   3 check   8 flight
   4 course   9 Welcome
   5 together   10 front
2 1 d   2 c   3 b   4 e   5 f   6 a
3 1 Could I see your boarding pass, please?
   2 Would you put your bag in the overhead locker, please?
   3 Could you switch off your phone now, please?
   4 Can I ask what your seat number is, please?
   5 Would you sit there, please?
   6 Would you mind folding your tray table, please?
4 1 Is it possible to change seats with someone near us?
   2 Because everyone is boarding just now.
   3 four seats together
   4 three rows behind us
   5 Because the new seat is also an aisle seat. She says 'I want an aisle seat, too.'
5 1 how   6 volume
   2 menu   7 reading
   3 down   8 press
   4 select   9 button
   5 then
6 1 carefully   7 pulling
   2 instruction   8 lift
   3 familiarize   9 throughout
   4 board   10 pointed
   5 sign   11 nearest
   6 buckle   12 open
7 1 Please fasten your seatbelt, sir. (h)
   2 Please put your seat in the upright position. (g)
   3 Can I just check your seatbelt? (f)
   4 Would you mind switching off your computer? (e)
   5 Please switch off your phone. (d)
   6 Could you put your table up, sir? (c)
   7 Would you mind putting your bag in the overhead locker? (a)
   8 Please read this notice. (b)

Self Study 3

1
1 shortly
2 through the cabin
3 light refreshments
4 Kindly
5 menu card
6 exact change
7 a short flight
8 remain seated

2 Ladies and **gentlemen**, it's great **to** have you on board. The seatbelt sign has been switched **off**. You **can move** around the cabin now. In a few moments we shall be **coming** through **the** cabin with refreshments. Please be ready **with** your order. We'd really appreciate **it** if you had the exact change for your purchases.

3
1 sign
2 short
3 service
4 minutes
5 time
6 seated
7 aisles
8 trolleys

4
1 immediately after the seatbelt sign is off
2 50 minutes / less than an hour
3 remain seated
4 moving in the aisles
5 get the trolleys out to begin the refreshment service

5
1 Of course, no problem at all. I'll be right back.
2 I'll be back with a new pair in a few minutes.
3 Let me get them a snack.
4 Just give me a few minutes to get that ready for you.

6
1 Don't
2 Let
3 all right
4 feeling
5 call
6 course
7 else
8 back
9 apologize
10 problem
11 ahead
12 help

7 Sentences 2, 5, and 6 (Sentence 1 would be said by a pilot or air traffic controller – it is not appropriate for passengers.)

Self Study 4

1
1 ask
2 menu
3 full
4 starter
5 course
6 much
7 pre-order
8 special
9 tray
10 choose

2 Starter: egg mayonnaise, smoked salmon, tuna salad, tomatoes and olives, salade niçoise, seafood salad
Main course: chicken tikka, fish in white sauce, beef bourguignon, lasagne, chicken satay and rice, lamb and couscous
Dessert: chocolate pudding, lemon sponge, fruit salad, apple pie, grapes, ice cream
Cheese and biscuits does not go in any of the columns.

3 Before the meal: 2, 6, 9, 13
During the meal: 1, 3, 8, 11, 12
After the meal: 4, 5, 7, 10, 14

4
1 What would you like to drink, madam?
2 Would you like something to drink, sir?
3 Would you care for a drink, sir?
4 What can I get you, sir?
5 Could I have a glass of water?
6 Can I have a cold beer, please?

5
1 d   2 f   3 a   4 g
5 b   6 e   7 h   8 c

6 Across 2 RAZOR   4 WHISKY   5 PERFUME   8 CHOCOLATES   9 VODKA   10 TEDDY
Down 1 CIGARS   3 AFTERSHAVE   6 MASCARA   7 JEWELLERY

Self Study 5

1
1 The cabin is too cold.
2 23°C
3 turn up the thermostat and give the passengers a blanket
4 20 minutes
5 beverage
6 a blanket
7 return to the couple five minutes later
8 a hot chocolate drink

2
1 Can I help you?
2 I'm really sorry.
3 Can I get you …?
4 I'll pop back to see you in about five minutes.
5 Would that be all right?

3
1 T   2 T   3 T   4 F   5 F   6 T
7 F   8 T   9 F

4
1 I'll check on our arrival time and get back to you.
2 I'll get it for you; I'll get it now.
3 I'll get you a blanket in the meantime; I'll be back in a moment.
4 I'll see what I can do; I'll ask if there is a doctor or nurse on board.

5   1 c   2 g   3 a   4 b   5 f   6 e   7 d

Self Study 6

1
1 turbulence
2 return
3 hurt
4 head
5 laptop
6 locker
7 unconscious
8 colleague
9 kit
10 opened
11 dizzy
12 pain
13 glass
14 cut
15 wound
16 dressing
17 compress
18 fine
19 seat
20 fastened

2 stethoscope, gloves, diarrhoea tablets, painkillers, bandages, compresses, antiseptic wipes, triangular bandages, scissors, wound dressings, safety pins, face masks

3 Possible order of actions to take:
1 f   2 h   3 e   4 c   5 b   6 d
7 i   8 j   9 k (if there is one)
Actions not to take: a, g, l

4 CHECK
1 How are you feeling?
2 Are you in pain?
8 Where's the pain?
11 Are you on any medication?
14 Have you been sick before?
CALL
3 He looks very sick.
5 He's not breathing normally.
9 He's complaining of a pain in his chest.
12 He says he's got chest pains.
CARE
4 Lie him down.
6 Make room please.
7 Get the oxygen and defibrillator.
10 Loosen his clothing.
13 Check his pulse.

5
1 collapsed
2 suffered
3 checked
4 loosened
5 asked
6 reported
7 administered
8 remained
9 arrived
10 recommended
11 decided

Self Study 7

1
1 emergency
2 locate
3 behind
4 exit
5 door
6 instructed
7 floor
8 guide
9 landing
10 adopt
11 vest
12 pressure
13 oxygen
14 compartment
15 flow
16 mouth
17 band
18 breathe
19 assistance
20 first

2
1 e   2 i   3 d   4 g   5 h   6 c
7 a   8 b   9 f

3
1 F   2 T   3 T   4 F   5 F   6 T
7 F   8 T   9 F   10 F   11 T   12 T

4 a 5   b 2   c 6   d 1   e 4   f 3

5 2 He told them to follow the instructions given to them by their crew.

3 He told them not to leave their seats until instructed.

4 He told them to make their way to the nearest exit.

5 He told the ladies to take off their high-heeled shoes.

6 He told them to leave all (their) personal belongings behind.

6 Suggested answer:

First of all, all the lights went off and the oxygen masks came down. Then there was a lot of smoke in the cabin and everyone was in a panic, but the cabin crew were very calm and told everyone to sit down. Then they shouted 'Go!' and we all rushed to the slides. I didn't have time to think about it or even take off my high-heeled shoes. Everyone was safe, but some people were injured at the bottom of the slides.

Self Study 8

1 1 c   2 b   3 b   4 a

2 1 f   2 a   3 e   4 d   5 b   6 c

3 1 need   6 change
2 standing   7 spare
3 folded   8 tell
4 upset   9 little
5 behind   10 fine

4 1 He has to ask the group to be quiet.

2 He asks them a 'special favour'.

3 No, they are quite pleasant.

4 Some passengers want to watch a film, others want to have a sleep.

5 They want another drink.

5 Sir, you have to stop shouting and you must **to** sit down, please. Madam, I can see how upset **you are**. Would you **come / mind coming** to the back of the plane with **me**, please? I **am** (or **do**) apologize, and please don't worry. Everything is **under** control and incidents like this are extremely rare.

6

A	B	U	S	I	V	E	D	M	E
C	G	R	F	S	H	A	I	Q	U
F	I	G	H	T	L	U	S	B	C
Z	C	E	R	I	E	R	R	O	W
U	L	M	B	E	F	O	U	Y	T
N	U	N	F	K	S	A	P	D	U
R	G	Y	K	R	B	S	T	P	E
U	P	S	H	O	U	T	I	N	G
L	X	H	A	Z	C	A	V	V	O
Y	N	W	I	J	L	A	E	D	E

Self Study 9

1 **20 minutes before landing**
1, 2, 6, 9, 11, 14
10 minutes before landing
4, 5, 7, 8, 10, 12
2 minutes before landing
3, 13

2 2 Fold it away, please.

3 Put them in the overhead lockers.

4 Switch it off now, please.

5 Put it upright, please.

6 Put it down, please.

3 1 to   5 eleven forty-five
2 4 o'clock   6 noon
3 takes   7 twenty-five to two
4 lasts   8 connecting

4 1 the time   4 When
2 time   5 how
3 how much   6 about

5 1 speaking   6 apologies
2 bad   7 inconvenience
3 Traffic   8 quickly
4 due   9 meantime
5 delayed   10 fastened

6 1 Have you done   4 Have they collected
2 Has she secured 5 Have you finished
3 Has he checked   6 Have we completed

7 1 flight deck   5 stowed
2 cabin crew   6 minute
3 checks   7 strapped
4 secure

Self Study 10

1 1 Have a wonderful holiday.

2 Enjoy your trip, madam.

3 Safe journey home.

4 Look forward to seeing you again soon.

5 I'm sorry it was such a bad flight.

6 Thank you for flying with us, sir.

7 Have a good day.
You would not normally use sentence 5.

2 1 I suggest (that) you don't wear

2 I suggest (that) you let

3 I suggest (that) you have

4 I suggest (that) you don't take

5 I suggest (that) you visit

3 1 behalf   8 remind
2 local   9 permitted
3 stowed   10 outside
4 off   11 should
5 ensure   12 off
6 luggage   13 wish
7 injury   14 journey

4 The flight attendant was very late getting strapped in for landing.

5 I shouldn't have got stuck dealing with that passenger. I should have acted more quickly.
You should all know that cabin crew must be strapped in for landing.
We should all know the procedures …
We should all be aware of possible problems …
… we should all be working for each other all the time.

6 1 You should've all known that cabin crew must be strapped in for landing.

2 We should've all known the procedures …

3 We should've all been aware of possible problems …

4 … we should've all been working for each other all the time.

7 2 ✓   3 ✓   5 ✓

8 Incorrect sentences:

2 You **shouldn't to open** the overhead lockers now.

3 You **shouldn't have got** involved in an argument with that passenger.

5 They **shouldn't to be going** to the toilets any more.

8 I should **to tell** the purser.

9 **Across** 4 GOODBYE   5 LANDING
6 NOISY   7 EMERGENCIES   9 TAKE OFF
10 DOCTOR   11 BRIEFING
Down 1 FOOD   2 COMPLAINTS
3 WELCOME   8 CAPTAIN